From Barren To Bearing

Power of a Testimony

GINA REDWOOD-LLOYD

GINA REDWOOD-LLOYD

FROM BARREN TO BEARING, Power of a Testimony by Gina Redwood-Lloyd

Although the author and publisher have made every effort to ensure that the information in this book was correct at press time, the author and publisher (Gina Redwood-Lloyd & DiViNE Purpose Publishing) do not assume and hereby disclaim any liability to any party for any loss, damage, or disruption caused by errors or omissions, whether such errors or omissions result from negligence, accident, or any other cause.

This publication contains the opinions and ideas of its author. Relevant laws vary from state to state. The strategies outlined in this book may not be suitable for every individual, and are not guaranteed or warranted to produce any particular results.

No warranty is made with respect to the accuracy or completeness of the information contained herein, and both the author and publisher specifically disclaim any responsibility for any liability, loss, or risk, personal or otherwise, which is incurred as a consequence, directly or indirectly, of the use and application of any of the contents of this book.

This book or parts thereof may not be reproduced in any form, stored in a retrieval system, or transmitted in any form by any means—electronic, mechanical, photocopy, recording, or otherwise—without prior written permission of the publisher/author, except as provided by United States of America copyright law.

Unless otherwise indicated, all Scripture quotations are taken from the Holy Bible, New Living Translation, copyright © 1996, 2004, 2007 by Tyndale House Foundation. Used by permission of Tyndale House Publishers, Inc., Carol Stream, Illinois 60188. All rights reserved.

Scriptures quotations marked (KJV) are taken from the Holy Bible, King James Version

"Scripture quotations taken from the Amplified® Bible,
Copyright © 1954, 1958, 1962, 1964, 1965, 1987 by The Lockman Foundation
Used by permission." (www.Lockman.org)

Published by DiViNE Purpose Publishing TM Printed by CreateSpace
Available from Amazon.com, CreateSpace.com, and other retail outlets

Copyright © 2015 Gina Redwood-Lloyd All rights reserved.

Library of Congress Control Number: 2015935888

ISBN-13: 978-0692405840 (DiViNE Purpose Publishing)

ISBN-10: 0692405844

Printed in the United States of America

~Reviews

Bless the Lord! "From Barren to Bearing-Power of a Testimony" by Gina Redwood-Lloyd, is a God-Send! From the moment I read the title, I knew that I was in for a treat from the Lord!

In nine power-pack chapters, (nine chapters to match that it take nine months to give birth!) The author has incredible wit and warmth in her writing! You remain engaged throughout each spectacular page! Gina unfolds not only her amazing, awe inspiring testimony, but essential Biblical principles, encouragement, and guidelines to get to the next dimension of our lives! I was able to gain so much insight and understanding by the words that God gave her to give to us! This book allowed me to reflect not only on the author's testimony, but even my own! It touched me in areas of my life that were dry and in need of quenching again! The chapters Physical and Financial Barrenness were especially needed as reminders of God's promises and His goodness and that He is just to reward those that diligent serve and have faith and trust in Him! And the instructions given on The Birthing Process will help you to accelerate your prayer and worship life and produce a bumper crop of fruit!!

"From Barren to Bearing, Power of a Testimony", is destined to bring forth deliverance, healing and transform lives for the Glory of God! This book is a must have for EVERY woman's arsenal no matter what her age! It addresses the Whole Woman, Mind, Body and Spirit!! I highly recommended every woman to get two copies, one for herself, and one for a friend! Thank you Gina Redwood-Lloyd for your obedience to the Lord in BIRTHING this moving book for the Women of God!

Sincerely,

Min. Tonya Cash

This book touches the heart on many levels. Christians have to guard against many things and learn to rely on God to help change their hearts if there is any malice within it. The words chosen are not only her testimony but words of love from God to a dying world. God doesn't want to see his people perish but to turn from their wicked ways and to keep their eyes on the prize. The prize being us with him in paradise for eternity. This book encourages us not to stay in a stagnant state where we are found in our Christianity and our relationship with God but to keep moving forward. This book helps us to renew our faith, to keep pressing in, to keep pushing forward and to keep pressing to be at the feet of our Heavenly Father. He doesn't want to leave us where we are, but wants to elevate us from level to level. So for every teenager, woman, and man that reads this book will not only reflect but will be given a measure of faith to continue to be in his presence.

Love,

Myra from Connecticut!

~~~~~~

"From Barren to Bearing" is a must read for females and males alike. It is filled with examples of life trials and mixed with the practical application of scriptures to build your faith. It demonstrates the love and power of God and the power of forgiveness. So you think your situation is unique? Yes, it is and this book is designed to create in you the power to believe and press through and trust the God, who will fight for you. Thank you Regina for keeping it real and sharing your life.

~Deramon Ann Murphy, MSW

The Potter's House International Ministries

In this book Author Gina Redwood –Lloyd endeavors to show how God can take the barrenness of any life situation and use it to heal, restore and bless you. Her example of Hannah, shows a woman who endured childlessness in a society where such was a curse. She dealt with ridicule and taunting and discouragement, yet trusted God for a man-child whom she dedicated to the service of the Lord in the temple; as a result of her faith, God blessed her with five other children (1Sam. 2:21). What a demonstration of God's grace!

Gina's story is riveting and sad yet powerful and exciting! Her experiences will have you captivated, picturing yourself in the midst her life. This book is a powerful testimony of God's power to save, heal and forgive; It shows that no matter what you may go through, God is able to redeem, turning it around for good. We appreciate the extensive use of the word of God for spiritual emphasis. You will find that Gina is painfully transparent. Nevertheless, she emerges victorious as one who submits to God's laws and precepts and statutes and commandments. Her theme or favorite saying, "He's a great big God that does great big things" epitomizes her story.

~Pastor Lester & LaVerne Walters

New Lighthouse Ministries, New Haven, CT.

~~~~~~

'From Barren To Bearing, Power of a Testimony' is transparent, thoughtful, and riveting. It's gives great insight into a life that can only be transformed by the power of prayer, honesty and integrity. Easy read.

~Olivia M. Roberts, MBA, MSLR.

~~~~~~

In "From Barren To Bearing" Gina Redwood-Lloyd gives you a front row seat to observe God's ongoing work in real life. The book is a candid and no holds barred look at her life and testimony and what God can do with even the the most wayward of lives. It should be an encouragement to anyone who feels that they are beyond God's working in their life. God can, and still does work miracles. Gina Redwood-Lloyd, is living proof.
~Tony Clarke

Foreword

The fruit of the Spirit is nine attributes of the Holy Spirit that we as Christian believers should display every day. It's a reflection to the world that we have been changed or transformed from our sinful nature to a renewed life with Christ. It's a must have throughout our entire Christian journey because it helps in areas like building our faith and character.

Love is a word that is used very carelessly in these days and times. We say it without any understanding of the word. Love is not an emotion, it's an act. It's patient and kind, never jealous or envious, never boastful or proud, never haughty, selfish or rude. You're not quickly upset with someone you love. They may have ways about them that are not so lovable, but love will love them still. Love will help the unlovable become lovable, so that others will love on them. In that we see the act of kindness being shown. We're supposed to be helpers to one another anyway, but when we help the ones we love it creates a special bond between the persons. Love does not resent or envy another for their achievements, but genuinely congratulates the person and is happy for them.

We live in a society that will actually kill over something that belongs to someone else because in their mind they think they deserve it. And yes, it'll most likely be the one that supposed to have your back. The very one that calls you every day just to check up on you and to tell you that they love you. Yup! Those would be the ones. In the same breath they're boasting about all the things that they have that you don't have, trying to make you feel like the lesser person. The fact of the matter is that they're the ones who is scheming on the little that you have and is trying to keep from having anything else of value. They are also the same ones who will not ask for your help when they are in a bind, because in their mind you are beneath them. They can't let you in on what's really going on in their home because they have to keep up this front to say they got it going on. Then when you do get wind of it and try to offer help they turn it down because they know that if the shoe were on the other foot they wouldn't help you.

That is not love. Love will do just the opposite. Love is very courteous and will not be ill mannered towards you, but will treat you with dignity and respect. When you love someone, what they say or do from time to time will not irritate you and make you touchy towards them. Every time they say certain things it pricks that spot that makes you almost sick to your stomach.

We see this a lot of times in relationships when we're in them for all the wrong reasons. The person can't come near you to hug you, hold your hand, or even kiss you because you haven't had time to work yourself up for it. But yet and still you will demand all the things you'd like done in the relationship that will make you comfortable in it. That means you could only love under your conditions which isn't love at all. Love will love you under any condition, that's what makes it unconditional. Love will also forgive and move on. We have to stop holding these grudges toward one another. It's like a terminal disease eating us up inside. It even at times causes physical disease that leads to death. The bible requires us to forgive even our enemies, so why not someone we call friend, sister/brother in Christ? Jesus forgives us over and over again with love and compassion in His heart. We must learn how to be more Christ like and this is why the fruit of the Spirit is so important. And just to be clear, we are commanded to love and where love lives hate cannot rent space there.

I love the scripture in Psalm 30:5 where it says "Weeping may endure for a night but joy cometh in the morning." But what about when you have to have joy during the storm? Opposition is coming from every angle and the pressure of it is weighing you down. Satan is whispering in one ear that you won't make it through this one, it's too much for you to bear. And God on the other had is reminding you of the promises He made to you. How many of you know that it's right there in that very moment a joy comes up from the pit of your belly that lets you know that it's already alright and its working for your good. Before you know it, in that joy you feel a peace, that peace that passeth all understanding, that peace that keeps our hearts and minds through Christ Jesus. You yourself don't understand it beyond the fact that it's the peace of God because what you're facing should have you somewhere on some type of anti-depressant. But God!

Your faith will begin to build as you remember what God said verses what the devil is saying that will take you into the deep. You'll find your prayer life increasing and your plate being turned down in fasting all because you believe. You're focused on God and you're ready to hear and follow His instructions so that you could indeed give birth to the promises He has made in your life.

Preface

I remember the day in May of 2014, God gave me a vision. The vision was of a woman that looked like one of the women on the cover of the book *'The Bible Story'* that I use to read as a child. The woman's dress was blue and red with a red sash and a white covering over her head as they use to wear in the bible days. At first I couldn't figure out what God was trying to show me, and I didn't remember the story books at that time. But as soon as God dropped it into my spirit that the woman was from that book, I immediately started looking to see if a woman dressed as I describe was on the cover of one of those books. Since the number three is one of the numbers God deals with me on, it was only in line for me to find the woman on the cover of Volume III of the story books. I said to my husband that I believed it was Rachel with her son Joseph, and then we thought of Sarah as well as Hannah. But as I began to dwell on these three women, the Lord brought to my remembrance that they were all barren until God opened their womb to bear a child. It was in that moment that God gave me the name *'From Barren to Bearing'* as the title of a book. It was shortly after that the From Barren to Bearing Women's Ministry came about, and I am looking forward to whatever else God has in store for this ministry that He has birthed through me.

~ Acknowledgements ~

I would first like to acknowledge the Lord Jesus Christ, my Lord and Savior for impregnating me with this book. I could not have come up with such an idea and name of a book that will impact the lives of people all over the world.

Secondly I would like to acknowledge my wonderful husband who I love dearly, Apostle Garrett Lloyd who supports and believes in me and the God that works through me.

I'd like to acknowledge my children, Celeste Redwood, Erica Redwood-Kirk, Michael Williams, and Jean-Guy Charles for trusting the God in their mommy when we faced life's challenging moments. You fasted and prayed with me and saw the remarkable hand of God move in our lives. I love you.

I also would like to acknowledge all who have been a corner stone in my life over the years. Each one of you have played a big part in my life at one point or the other, encouraging me, praying for me, pushing me, loving me, and teaching me. Lester & Laverne Walters, Tony & Rosey Clarke, Olivia M. Roberts, Jackie Beckford, Mother Sis Beckford, Deramon Murphy, Clayton Lamont Gilliams, and my bestest friend ever, Myra Maldonado, a thousand thanks to each and every one of you.

~Dedication~

This book is dedicated to every person who has experienced barrenness in the different areas of their lives. I know that your health report is saying that you'll never recover, and your bank account is in the negative. I know that you're single and desiring a spouse or married and your marriage is in need of a love resuscitation. Wherever you fall in at, just know that with God you are able to produce or to produce again!

~ Table of Contents ~

Chapter 1
Barrenness
15

Chapter 2
Spiritual Barrenness
Forgiveness
Relationships
20

Chapter 3
Bearing Purpose
37

Chapter 4
Financial Barrenness
The Tither
The Trust
The Test
46

Chapter 5
Prayer, Faith, & Fruition
62

Chapter 6
Good Seeds/Bad Seeds
73

Chapter 7
Physical Barrenness
81

Chapter 8
The Fruit Bearer
90

Chapter 9
The Birthing Process
Active Labor
Pushing
Delivering the Placenta
98

Barrenness

Chapter 1

When you are physically barren you're not able to produce children. When you are spiritually barren you're not able to produce or bear what God has impregnated you with. So in order to bear forth good fruit, your seed must fall into good ground according to God's word.

Matthew 13:8 - "But other fell into good ground, and brought forth fruit, some an hundredfold, some sixtyfold, and some thirtyfold".

Having good ground requires work and it's not going to feel good. God would need to cultivate our inner man with His spiritual tools like the garden rake to break up the hardened soil in our lives like un-forgiveness, past hurts and pain, rejection, etc., and then level them out with healing, peace, forgiveness, and love. Another tool would be the garden hoe which is used for weeding up the bad habits in our life and exposing them in an anointed atmosphere in the presence of the Holy Ghost for deliverance. There are other tools that God uses, but let's look at the grounds of some of the barren women in the bible.

Sarah, Abraham's wife fertilized her ground with faith and trust. She believed in what God said. However, somewhere down the road she allowed the weed of confusion to spring up before her name changed.

Genesis 16:2 - "And Sarai said unto Abram, Behold now, the Lord hath restrained me from bearing: I pray thee, go in unto my maid; it may be that I may obtain children by her. And Abram hearkened to the voice of Sarai."

Did God not say to Abraham in ***Genesis 15:4*** that Eliezer wasn't going to be his heir, but he that shall come forth out of thine own bowels? Sarah, when did God ever change his mind? And are we not the same way? God tells us something specific and because it's not happening the way we thought it should be happening, we try to twist what was clearly spoken. It's no wonder why we find ourselves in a mess that was never meant for us to go through. The bible tells me this:

"Numbers 23:19 - God is not a man, that he should lie; neither the son of man, that he should repent: hath he said, and shall he not do it? Or hath he spoken, and shall he not make it good?"

If He (God) said it, He will do it. In other words, His word is good and we can bank on it. Confusion came to Sarah's house when she suggested to her husband to have sex with her maid and have a child with her. She indicated that maybe that would be the way God would bless them with a son. In the meantime, Hagar is pregnant and can't stand you and you want to place all the blame on Abraham for what you started. Yes, he was at fault as well because he listened to what his wife said instead of reminding her of what God said. But indeed it was time for Sarah to pull up those weeds of confusion because God said that He is not the author of it! But I love how Abraham handled the situation. He said (paraphrasing), that's your maid, and your mess, deal with it as you please, the ball is in your court! We sometimes do have to deal with the monsters that we've created. Repent and stand up to it and allow the spirit of correction to come in and set things back in order so that your ground may be good once more.

Like most born again believers, our waiting season tend to be the worst season ever. Because we live in an age where everything happens right now, right away, and on the dime, we don't want to wait for God's perfect timing because it doesn't fit into our schedules. For example, we get a word of prophecy that our husband/wife is going to enter our lives soon. You will be in ministry together and will travel the world spreading the gospel of Jesus Christ. Now, here is what happens....As soon as we get home we have our computers up, calculators out, and our list of names. The computer is to tell everyone on social media that we're getting married, the calculator is to calculate how much the wedding will cost, and the list is of persons we feel may or may not be the one. Help us Jesus! And then we go around saying something like this; in six months I'm going to get married to a great man/woman of God and we're going to travel the world together preaching the gospel of Jesus Christ. I even think I know who the person is.... The Lord spoke it over my life! And then the person you're talking to is asking; "So God told you in six months all these things will happen and you think you know who it is?"

And then you reply; "Well, He didn't say six months, but He knows that I can't wait that long....I'm over ready!"

Now, here comes the mess. I've also been having a little thing for Minister so and so, so I think they just may be the one. After wheeling them in, you and Minister so and so start dating. You see the signs of destruction, but won't get out of it and repent because you must meet "your timing." So, you stay in the relationship and get married six months later convinced that you're in the will of God. Two months later your marriage is falling apart because "things just aren't working out all of a sudden." You don't want to admit that the signs were there before saying "I do." Now your God ordained spouse shows up in your life and becomes your sister or brother in Christ. They can't be no more than that because you're married, hurt, confused, and angry with God because you didn't wait on His perfect timing. And here's another example!

God said that He was going to heal your body of that cancer that has been eating away at it. You cried tears of joy, you rejoiced in what was said. You even said it yourself, "I am healed" in Jesus name! You've walked in your faith believing God during your whole treatment. But now you've gone through the chemo and your pet scan results showed that the cancer is still there. Not only is it still there, it has in fact spread! All of a sudden doubt begins to creep in…You're saying to yourself things like, "Maybe God meant that I'll be healed through death." The cancer has spread to the liver and the doctor said that they can give more chemo, but the chances of surviving this are slim to none. What happened right there was this. You couldn't see your body being healed without the treatments helping it. You forgot about God being your healer and the great Physician because you weren't healed when you were expected to be healed which was after your chemo. But as it was said to Abraham Sarah's husband; "Is there anything too hard for the Lord!"

Now, imagine if we had to wait as long as Sarah did? She waited so long for her promise that the weed of doubt rose up in her good ground.

Genesis 18:10-12 reads; [The Lord] said, I will surely return to you when the season comes round, and behold, Sarah your wife will have a son. And Sarah was listening and heard it at the tent door which was behind Him. 11) Now Abraham and Sarah were old, well advanced in years; it had ceased to be with Sarah as with [young] women. [She was past the age of childbearing]. 12) Therefore Sarah laughed to herself, saying, After I have become aged shall I have pleasure and delight, my lord (husband), being old also? Amp version

Sarah saw where she was at that time of her life and couldn't see beyond it at that moment. She was past the childbearing stage and probably thought to herself that she missed God somewhere along the way. She probably just gave up all hope like most of us do. But because it's not about us, but about the miracle God wants to perform through us…, He will restore our faith in a moment's time, pulling out those weeds of doubt by saying,

At the time appointed I will return unto thee, according to the time of life, and Sarah shall have a son. (Genesis 18:14)

So, at the appointed time in your life, He will make good on His word. Sarah gave birth to Isaac at the appointed time and the word of God was fulfilled.

Spiritual Barrenness

Chapter 2

Have you ever experienced a time in your Christian walk where you couldn't pray or read your bible? Something may have troubled you and in return affected your spirit which offset your mindset. It put you in a place where you're no longer thinking about things above, but about the situation that have now depressed and oppressed you. And although you've tried, you just can't seem to snap back from it. Well guess what? That is what we call spiritual barrenness. You can't sing and you have no joy because of what you allowed to block your womb of spiritual fruitfulness. But in **Isaiah 54:1** it tells us to break forth into singing! Sometimes you just have to open your mouth even when you don't want to or feel like it, and break out with a song. You're entitled to your joy, peace, and happiness! This is one of the many reasons why we must pray for the spirit of discernment. It would benefit us greatly if we could discern at the beginning of a situation that Satan wants to kill our dreams, steal our joy, and destroy our life. We could then prevent spiritual barrenness by speaking to the situation with God's word.

I remember going through spiritual barrenness at a church I was once attending. I was the choir director and one of the praise and worship leaders and loved all of what I did for the glory of God. The problem was that the keyboardist and I could never seem to be on the same page at one time which stirred up a lot of confusion. He could never catch the concept of me being the director and he the musician, or perhaps him following my leadership. But to be a great leader you must first learn how to follow, and as a leader you must learn how to take the advice of others into consideration…, something we should always remember. You see, it wasn't about me being in leadership, but about me keeping my promise to God to never say no to whatever I'm asked to do for the Kingdom.

I never wanted to be a choir director, I was appointed choir director and then went on to be a praise and worship leader. But in any case, because we couldn't see eye to eye it caused resentment to build up between the both of us. And because his mother was the pastor and his grandfather the Bishop, I felt like if I had made a complaint against him it would not have been any real justice. Indeed I should have consulted God on the matter, but instead I had gotten angry and decided that I wasn't going back to church ever again. I was still a young babe in Christ, so my boyfriend at the time was still present in my life, and of course that's who Satan placed before me as a comforter in the dissension. After all, I was hurting and no one else seemed to care. So instead of going to church that Sunday, I spent the weekend at his house. Did it feel good being in his arms? Yes. But the devil always presents things as being good, or feeling good….. But are they really good for you?

After indulging in the act of fornication, that morning I decided to watch my boyfriend work in the yard from the balcony that was off of the master bedroom. But as soon as I got to the door I saw the next door neighbor and tried to ease back inside. We had gotten well acquainted with one another when I use to live there, and trust me, I did not want her to see me. She was one of those up in age God fearing Jamaican women that didn't play…lol.

Anyway, she saw me and beckon for me to come over. When I finally got to her yard I asked why she wasn't in church and she replied that she wasn't feeling well. Then she turned around and asked me the very same question and my response was that I was done with church. Why did I say that? The woman began to minister from her heart to me in love while standing out there in her driveway. My soul was so convicted that tears started streaming down my face and in my heart I began to repent. In that moment I was set free of my spiritual barrenness because my spirit was open to receive the healing that it had needed to move forward. There was no way I would have been able to stay in that place if I wanted to continue sowing into others what was birthed through me. The gift of teaching choirs not only how to sing their different parts and breathe through them, but how to sing from a place of worship with a clean and pure heart that would allow them to minister verses just singing.

The next Sunday I went to church with joy in my heart and a praise on my lips. The battle was never mine, but the Lord's. God had already worked it out! I didn't even have to mention the problem to the pastor, someone else discussed it with her and she took care of it. The love I felt from her on that day from the pulpit was well accepted and appreciated. Justice that day was in the camp.

Isaiah 54:4 - Fear not, for you shall not be ashamed; neither be confounded and depressed, for you shall not be put to shame. For you shall forget the same of your youth, and you shall not [seriously] remember the reproach of your widowhood any more. Amp version

Forgiveness

Being spiritually barren also puts a person in a state of not being able to bear the fruit of the spirit which is love, joy, peace, long-suffering, gentleness, goodness, faith, meekness, and temperance. *(Galatians 5:22-23)* As I mentioned earlier in this chapter, I found myself fornicating. I was operating out of my flesh because my heart wasn't right. I allowed my emotions to run away with me because I was hurt. What if I would have waited a little longer on God to take care of the situation? I probably would not have fell into sin. I know that most of us have experienced some kind of hurt during our Christian walk, it will happen sooner or later. But we as Christians so often make the mistake of acting out of our feelings instead of taking it into prayer. We dwell on the problem and allow things like anger and hatred to set in which leads to greater problems like retaliation. When we get to the point of wanting to repay someone of the wrong that they have done to us, we have allowed not only anger and hatred to set in, but now un-forgiveness.

Let me share this testimony with you. As a child, like so many other children, I went through molestation. Around the age of twelve or thirteen years old I decided to inform my mother that I was being molested by her husband, my stepfather, with the hope that she would put a stop to it. She did come up with a plan..., she decided to take care of it by asking our next door neighbor if I could stay at their house after school until she came home from work. I indeed followed her instructions to stay next door until she came home, but at the same time anger and resentment began to set into my heart against her because I didn't feel as though she handled it well. I was still being violated by him whenever she wasn't around. In my opinion she should have kicked him out of our house because it wasn't a home as long as he was there. However, I think I understood her thought process. It didn't make any of it right, but she did have thirteen children and my stepfather was the father of none of us. She appeared to have been in survival mode. I rationalize it like this; He had a great job and was a true provider, and she couldn't see how to make it without him even though at the time it was only three of us left at home.

Although I came to that conclusion, I still carried this anger with me well into my adulthood...even into my Christian walk long after my stepfather passed away. I do thank God that he apologized to me years before his passing, but until this very day, my mother does not acknowledge it. All she acknowledges is that he was a good man, a good husband, and a great provider. Now, can you imagine how hard it was for me when God said I had to forgive her? I was going about my Christian walk just fine without a thought, negative or positive, of her. In fact, I thought it was all good in the eyesight of the Lord seeing that I said nothing good or evil about her, but little did I know.... ~smiles~ I struggled with it to be very honest, but pleasing God was definitely more important to me than holding a grudge.

One day not too long after the revelation, I picked up the phone and called my mom. To my surprise we had a very long conversation about the wonders of God our savior. It was very enlightening! After a while I started calling her on a regular basis and it felt great! I was going through my deliverance! It wasn't about her at all; it was about me forgiving her even though she never said "I'm sorry." It was about the matter of the heart, my heart.

After moving to Georgia, I was able to visit her more often seeing that I'm closer to where she lives now, something I dreaded when I was in the state of un-forgiveness. I'm no longer barren in that area, but I am free to love! I found peace in the whole situation, its joyful whenever I'm speaking to her or going to visit, and I'm able to show her love, goodness, and kindness from my heart. Meekness was displayed when God gave me the patience and tolerance to deal with it all without losing my temper. I now have the faith that God can restore families and will show them who you really are in Him if they should have ever doubted.

For instance, during one of my visits at my mother's house, one of my sisters wanted to start an argument with me. She came through the door fussing and carrying on, but yet I remained calm. When she finally realized that I wasn't going to fuss and fight with her as I would have normally done, she began bringing up things from my past. And if that wasn't enough, I heard for the first time a lie that she started about me throughout the family. But that was okay because most of all, she finally gave me an understanding of how she really felt about me as children growing up unto this day. She too held anger and resentment in her heart, but it was towards me. It was shocking to say the least! But knowing how I affected her life gave me the opportunity to apologize, to say that I was sorry for hurting her. It also gave me the chance to explain to her that I was going through molestation at that particular time, which is no excuse, but the anger of it had me acting out. I explained about that day she was talking and laughing at me with her friends when we were younger that resulted in me beating her up and saying mean things to her as children. I felt as though I was doing all I could do to protect her, so that this man wouldn't touch her as he did to a few of our sisters before me. And in my eyes she repaid me by looking at me as if I was the culprit that made our family so dysfunctional. But if she could only open her heart to forgiveness, it would be a beginning ground for healing to take place within her. After all, it wasn't her fault that our mother had her believing that I was crazy and delusional regarding my accusation against my stepfather. In all that happened on that day, God got the glory.

My other sister who witnessed the disturbance as well as my mom and others that were present was able to see the God in me. My mother's exact words were, "I know Gina has changed." And my older sister said, "It was like Gina was the angel and the other sister the devil." The fruit of the Spirit was once again displayed and God got the glory out of it all. It was a moment where I too had to look back and say to myself that some years back I would have reacted differently… But God! And although my sister and I have not resolved our issue as of yet, my heart is right towards her and I'm praying that God restores our relationship as he did with me and our mother. My faith is definitely activated in that area.

We should never dwell on our problems. It's an open door for Satan to break us down and destroy our spirit man.

Relationships

I know you must be saying "What does spiritual barrenness have to do with relationships." Well, sharing your body with someone who is not your spouse is very detrimental to your spirit man. Every time you have sex with that person, you take on a part of their spirit. Sex was design for marriage.

Mark 10:6-9 But from the beginning of the creation God made them male and female. 7) For this cause shall a man leave his father and mother, and cleave to his wife; 8) And they twain shall be one flesh: so then they are no more twain but one flesh. 9) What therefore God hath joined together, let not man put asunder.

After the passing of my first husband I began to date. The first man I dated wasn't someone that I was in love with, just a friend who I thought I could eventually love who helped me through my husband's death. However, our relationship resulted in us having a child out of wedlock that I will touch on later in this book. But the relationship I want to discuss right now is the second one I was involved in after the passing of my first husband. I thought that I was in love all over again! He was tall, brown skinned, handsome, and spoke French, the language of love. He swept me off my feet with his charm and smooth disposition he had about himself, and the expensive gifts didn't hurt any. I was young and inexperienced and he knew it. Everything he said was everything I wanted to hear, and in my mind I thought that he could very well be my next husband. And although I didn't give into him sexually right away, a few months later when I did was the start of another soul tie. All of my feelings and emotions were in this relationship because it felt right, until I got pregnant. That pregnancy definitely played as the downfall of that relationship. And I use the term "played as" because the foundation of it wasn't built on good grounds. There were a lot of missing additives, the main one being Jesus Christ. He was so shallow and vain and I couldn't see it because I chose to be blind to it. He didn't want to take me anywhere anymore when I began to show because my coco cola bottle shape was gone.

Now let me help someone right here: Love is not ashamed of you. Love will love you no matter how big or little you or your wallet may have gotten. But then again, true love is found in Christ, so if they are not in Him, how could they possibly know how to love, be in love or be loved….. But I wasn't saved then so work with me. He started seeing someone else on the side and even met up with her at his sister's wedding that he brought me to! Of course I didn't know it then that they were seeing each other behind my back, but I sensed it that night. And to make it real clear, when the reception was over he offered to take her back to wherever she was staying. But instead of dropping her and the other people off first and us going home together, he took me home first. Needless to say he didn't come back home until the next day and then feed me a big fat lie. In my heart I didn't believe it, but I accepted it because I thought I was in love and I didn't want anything to jeopardize our "happy" home. And let me add, being in a relationship that isn't joined together by marriage will have your mind entrapped to thinking that you are a family because the concept of one is present. We see you the man, you the woman, and (child) children all living in one household and become deceive. The fact of it all is that you have nothing more than a huge mess because neither one have committed themselves to saying "I do" to each other. A husband, wife, and children make a family so let's not get that twisted or confused.

After I had the baby, my life with my half live in and half living out boyfriend became more miserable. He was now spending weekends out of the house and still holding on to his apartment although we were living together at mine. Another red flag, but I knew at this point that he was cheating on me with the woman from the wedding reception which was his sister's best friend. I chose not to accuse him of it but to say just enough to let him know that I was on to him hoping that he would stop. I used caution because I knew that if I ever made up in my mind to catch him in the act that I would leave him for good. That was one bridge that I wasn't ready to cross. My soul was entangled with his, so what was wrong from the start seemed right in the right now which made it hard to let go.

The time came where I was just tired of it all and made up in my mind to catch him and cut the relationship off. My spirit was damaged, I was broken, my heart was hurting and I was now ready to seek revenge. There's a saying about a women scorned that isn't so sweet, but let me show you where being out of the will of God will take you. It wasn't just him that I wanted to pay back, but his sister as well. She knew all along that he was cheating on me with her best friend. I actually overheard a conversation of hers saying that she liked her friend better for her brother than me, and had no problem talking about me like I was nothing. She thought that I had left the house that we were all at, but I came back to get the baby's bottle and overheard everything. The door was open, but I never went back in. I walked away with tears in my eyes along with a hurting heart. I had shown nothing, but love towards her and the family... I felt betrayed.

However, it didn't give me the right to do what I did in my mission of retaliation, killing two birds with one stone as the saying goes. I made advances towards her husband who thought he had the opportunity to prey on an inexperienced heartbroken young woman. Little did he know, he was a part of my plot to get revenge. He took the bait as I knew he would, and I started my journal. I noted the days he would leave his job and come over my house while his brother-in-law was working and his wife at home taking care of the children just to have sex with me. After the act he would lay there telling me the details of how they plotted against me to get my boyfriend and his wife's friend hooked up behind my back. I was Delilah in her rare form. He even gave me other information that I could use to hurt them both, at the appointed time I would break the news.

When my month long affair was over I decided to catch my boyfriend in the act and dissolve the relationship. June 28, 1997, the night Holyfield and Tyson would be fighting was the night I set out to catch him. I knew he would be at his apartment watching the fight supposedly with his cousin, but I saw right into that. Because he thought he knew me so well, he never expected for me to come to his apartment. I was obviously on a mission that he had no idea of and stood there with boldness as I knocked on his apartment door. When he opened the door all dressed up, I could see straight into the living room where the woman was sitting on the sofa dressed up as well and ready to go out. They must have had plans to go out after the fight, but I had a fight of my own and losing was not an option. I looked straight in his eyes and said to him in a soft low tone voice to come and get his things out of my house. He saw a look that he never saw before in my eyes and knew it was over between us. He made a scene after trying to talk to me and even raised his voice, but my mind was made up. His words could no longer penetrate my heart because it was now filled with anger, hurt, and retaliation. I never knew before then that I could be so deceitful, but the bible says this:

Jeremiah 17:9 – The heart is deceitful above all things, and desperately wicked: who can know it?

My heart was set out to do evil towards him and his sister and there was no way of talking me out of it. The relationship at the point was over and I never looked back.

In August of that same year I met my second husband dressed in all white at a grocery store. On December 6, 1997 we were married for all of the wrong reasons. My husband was well aware that I wasn't over my ex because we discussed it, but here I go again. I'm bringing up my second marriage because it was in this marriage that I announced my affair to my ex and his sister. Everything in my world was great at that time. My husband and I was about to close on our big beautiful home, and I was driving my brand new Honda Civic that the new husband had just purchased for me. It was now time for phase two of my fruitless plan of revenge.

Now we all know people who can't hold water as they say, and my ex-boyfriend's cousin and his girlfriend were those type of people. I went to them after work one day and told them I had had an affair with his cousin in law and that they shouldn't say anything, I had just needed to vent. I knew that before the day was over the news would be worldwide no matter how much they said they would keep my "secret," and it was. Before the week was over I was approached by both, my ex and his sister. I had the opportunity to proudly tell them about the affair with boldness. Their reaction gave me a moment's worth of joy, literally. I was so caught up on getting revenge that I didn't see what it would do to me in the long run. I was living in a spiritually barren place and didn't know it because I didn't know Christ.

I was experiencing false love, false joy, false peace, etc., and I kept experiencing it until I accepted the Lord as my personal savior in February of 2004. I then put to death my fleshly desire of fornication in July of 2006. No, it didn't happen for me over night, but I believe it could have happened sooner if I had the proper leaders to take me through deliverance because my heart was right, ripe, and ready. It was only at that time that I became teachable of how to become a virtuous woman. I dated no one through that process and remained before God seeking His face day and night. I lived this part of

1 Corinthians 7:34 - *The unmarried woman careth for the things of the Lord, that she may be holy both in body and in spirit*.

It's not enough to just be saved, but you must have the Holy Ghost. The Holy Ghost is a teacher and He will teach you as He taught me in this area of my life of how to get rid of all soul ties and become a woman in waiting. I must say that the reward was great. I am now in a fruitful marriage to a mighty man of valor and we are doing great things in the Kingdom of God for His glory. I thank God that I never allowed for my heart to get so bitter again. Even after giving my life to the Lord, my wrongful act bothered me. Of course I asked God for forgiveness, but I couldn't rest until I asked for their forgiveness.

It was easy for me to apologize to my ex-boyfriend because we had to keep in close communication for our son's sake. But it was a task to catch up with his sister. I didn't have her number anymore and they would never open the door for me if I went to her house. But God is so good, He saw fit to bring us together at a school's graduation. My daughter and her nephew was graduating high school and I saw her and her husband. I had heard that she'd gave her life to Christ as well, so that made it a bit easier for me to approach them both and apologize. What a weight that was lifted off of my shoulders!

Bearing Purpose

Chapter 3

    Never think that what you are going through is in vein. God's plan is always strategically orchestrated for His purpose in our lives. Have you ever been connected to someone you thought served you no purpose at all? Yet, later on down the road they were the connector who connected you to who you had needed to be connected with for the purpose of a project, a job, or spouse? Your destiny had no meaning until the person stepped into your life and made it come to life. Ruth the Moabite woman in the bible was married to Mahlon, Elimelech and Naomi son for about 10 years and they had no children. **(Ruth 1:4)** I'm sure most of us have never thought about Ruth not having any children by her first husband. But yes, she too was barren until God decided to open her womb. What impressed me the most about Ruth was her obedience, humbleness, faithfulness, meekness, and her teachable spirit.

She also had a certain respect for her mother-in-law that was outstanding! Naomi was a woman of God who must have displayed the character of God before her family and daughter-in-laws for them to honor her in the way that they did. Even when she told her daughter-in-laws to go back to their homes they refused until the second request came from Naomi. Orpah went back, but Ruth stayed. In fact, she clave to her mother-in-law and said;

Ruth 1:16-17 Intreat me not to leave thee, or to return from following after thee: for whither thou goest, I will go; and where thou lodgest, I will lodge: thy people shall be my people, and thy God my God: 17) Where though diest, will I die, and there will I be buried: the Lord do so to me, and more also if ought but death part thee and me. KJV

Looking at Ruth's character, I don't think she regrets being married to Mahlon so many years without giving birth to a child. Her heart probably ached for a child like most barren women, but I believe she kept hoping while loving and honoring her husband throughout the years. You have to remember, women in those days thought their world ended, figuratively speaking, when they didn't bear a child, especially a boy child. I also don't believe she knew what being connected to her husband would have connected her to in the future! All she knew at this point was that her husband was gone and she didn't want to be disconnected to the closest thing to him, her mother-in-law and the God that lived through her. I know that we Christians today think that we know what's best for us, even more so than God. When we are connected to people who genuinely have the heart of God, but are yet different in ways like personalities, status in life, or backgrounds, we tend to shun them. Some of us nourish the person with love, patience and understanding as I believed Naomi did with her daughter-in-laws who were Moabites.

Then there are others who talk down to them, made them feel unimportant as well as unwanted within the body of Christ because of where they came from. We say to ourselves that there's no way God could have placed such a person in my life. God is saying, "If you could just look past the surface, pass the way they look, or where they come from, I can bless you beyond measure." Naomi looked past who Ruth was and they both were blessed through the process of it all. I could only imagine how Ruth's family and friends must have felt about her leaving her country. Some probably said she wouldn't make it and others probably laughed at her saying that she was crazy, while friends turned their backs. When we're walking with God, it causes us most of the time to walk alone allowing God to place the right folks in our lives to guide us to our destiny.

Ruth was now around people that weren't of her own kind, but she didn't allow that to detour her from what needed to be done in the home. They were starting all over again and of course it wasn't easy. How do I know it wasn't easy? For the simple fact that she said this:

Ruth 2:2 - Let me go to the field and glean among the ears of grain after him in whose sight I shall find favor. Naomi said to her, Go, my daughter. KJV

Back in those days, if you had substantial income you wouldn't have to glean in someone's field. To glean means to gather grain or other material that is left after the main crop has been gathered. So, you know they were facing hard times for real, but Ruth was ready to go to work. Now because the favor of God was upon her life the bible says in **Ruth 2:3** that she just happened to stop at the part of the field belonging to Boaz, who was of the family of Elimelech. Now look at what happened!

Ruth 2:4 - And behold, Boaz came from Bethlehem and said to the reapers, The Lord be with you! And they answered him, The Lord bless you!

You mean to tell me that Boaz just so happened to come home right at the time Ruth was in his field? Only God! It's so important to be at the right place at the right time. But in order to do that, you have to be in right relationship with God. You must develop a relationship with Him through prayer, so that you will know His voice when He is speaking through and to you. God has a way of putting you in the spotlight when you are looking dim.

There was a time when I didn't have any food on my table to feed my four children. I was in obedience with God, faithful, humble, and in good communication with Him. I didn't call on people to help me, but I told Jesus my problems and in return He laid me on a sister in Christ heart. She said to me that while shopping God told her to buy some groceries for me. She too had a good relationship with God because she was able to hear His voice and her obedience to Him, caused for her to act upon it. The food filled my cabinets, refrigerator, and freezer!!! It was food in abundance! The same with Ruth…. She had been noticed by her blessing and found favor!

Ruth 2:5 Then said Boaz unto his servant that was set over the reapers, Whose damsel is this?

Listen, you never have to go searching for a blessing, God will either lead you to it or allow it to find you. We just have to be or remain in compliance with His word.

John 15:7 – If ye abide in me, and my words abide in you, ye shall ask what ye will, and it shall be done unto you. KJV

Ruth was now overtaken by favor all because Boaz heard about how she took care of his relative, Naomi, her mother-in-law after the death of her husband Elimelech. Boaz offered her to stay in his field and his field only close to his maidens. He offered protection so that the young men wouldn't rape her, then feed her, and then allowed her to glean amongst the bundle of grain stalk that were already tied together after reaping! Not only that, he ordered the men to even snap off some heads of barley and drop them on purpose for her to gleam that as well. I tell you, Ruth was set! She accepted the God of her mother-in-law and got to know Him for herself because she trusted Him.

Ruth 2:12 – The Lord recompense thy work, and a full reward be given thee of the Lord God of Israel, under whose wings thou art come to trust.

Now, although her blessing was present, it wasn't yet manifested. Ruth continued to work in the field unto the end of barley harvest *(the Jewish month of Nisan or April)* and wheat harvest *(the Jewish month of Sivan or the end of May going into June)* ***(Ruth 2:23)***. When we're in the right field of our promise, blessing, or God's strategic plan, favor surrounds us. But even in our time of favor we feel the pressure of what we're impregnated with which intrigues us to push until the manifestation births forth.

Naomi said to Ruth at the time appointed, the time of an open door, a window of opportunity as some may call it… Isn't it about time I try to find a husband for you so that you can be happily married again? The man I have in mind for you is Boaz who is a close relative. He'll be winnowing barely tonight at the threshing floor ***(Ruth 3:1-2)***.

Let's look at the words winnow and threshing floor for later references. Winnow means to remove things of less importance from your life or from a list of possible choices. Threshing floor scripturally is symbolic of the relationship between the Bride and the Bridegroom.

Remember, God always give instructions as He did through Naomi to Ruth. What is He instructing you to do? When Ruth was given her instructions ***(Ruth 3:3-4)***, she did not rebel or ask questions, she simply did as she was told. It was no wonder that Ruth came to Boaz at the threshing floor!

Boaz represents Jesus Christ our kinsman, our redeemer, and Ruth represents the Bride of Christ. She was able to remove or winnow every distraction from her mind, her thoughts, and her life that would hinder their connection, their union. She was fixated on her blessing and no one was going to talk her out of it or detour her from it. God can meet you there as well! He can wash and cleanse you and make you His own… All you have to say is "I do." I do accept you Jesus as my Lord and savior because I believe that you died for my sins, so that I may be saved.

After lying at Boaz feet asking him to honor his custom/culture by marrying her since he was a close relative, he was happy to oblige her. He and others watched her over a period of time and saw that she kept herself holy, she was a virtuous woman. Now the pressure of the push was when he told her there was another relative closer then him who can perform the part of a kinsman. But like Jesus tells us:

Matthew 6:34 – So do not worry or be anxious about tomorrow, for tomorrow will have worries and anxieties of its own. Sufficient for each day is its own trouble. AMP

Boaz told Ruth to fear not and don't worry because he will handle the matter. He said for her to lie down and rest until the morning. Without question Ruth laid at his feet. Allow me please to paint this picture for you. Boaz who is the representation of Jesus and Ruth who laid at his feet tells me this. When we are under the pressures of life, it's time to lay at the feet of Jesus and **P**ray **U**ntil **S**omething **H**appens! **P.U.S.H!**

The next day when Ruth returned home she did not return empty handed. Boaz sent her back with six measure of barley. Just like when we come out from being in the presence of the Lord, it's impossible to come out empty. Some of us come out with a seed planted in our womb, an idea or vision, or a word that will lead us into our destiny. After telling Naomi all that transpired the night before, Naomi was able to speak words of wisdom to Ruth by telling her to sit still and know that Boaz will not rest until he finishes the matter at hand that day. *(Ruth 3:18)* This is what we call the season of waiting. God is saying to you to be still and know that He is God. *(Psalm 46:10)* No good thing will He withhold from you. *(Psalm 84:11)* I, (God) is not a man that I should lie; neither the son of man that I should repent: If I said it, shall I not make it good? *(Numbers 23:19)* Does He not always come through for us? Don't worry about the ones who do not want you, or who have the means to help you, but choose not to because how they feel you should do things, etc. They don't understand what you're birthing! They weren't ordained to be the midwife and can't help you deliver anyway!

The Kinsman who was a closer relative to Naomi and Ruth than Boaz didn't want Ruth because of where she came from. It didn't matter that she gave her life to Christ and was living holy and sanctified before Him. All he saw was her past and declined the blessing, Ruth. But how about Boaz, the ordained one who was happy that he did! The purpose wasn't meant for the Kinsman and Ruth, but for Boaz and Ruth. That was in God's plan all along. And now watch what happened…

Ruth 4:13 – So Boaz took Ruth, and she was his wife; and when he went in unto her, the Lord gave her conception, and she bare a son.

You see, it was never meant for Ruth to bear a child with Mahlon. He was only the connection that connected her to the purpose, her destiny. And Naomi was the midwife that helped give birth to God's strategic plan.

Financial Barrenness

Chapter 4

If you have never driven down the road of lack, then consider yourself really blessed! But for those of us who have traveled down this road, we know that it's filled with pot holes of needs, desires, and wants. Regardless of how you got there, it will always be a difficult place to be in, but yet it's a place to learn and grow from, spiritually and naturally.

In October of 2006 I was homeless with four children to care for after resigning from my job. On September 26, 2006 God spoke one word to me audibly while sitting at my desk at work in the cancer center which was "Resign." I should have done it the day before after the dream He gave me when coming off of a seven day fast, but it didn't make sense to me. Why would God have me to leave my job knowing that I'm a single mom? And even more so, I loved my job! I loved praying for patients battling cancer and giving them encouraging words. So, the day before I went to the doctor I was assigned to at the time and said to her that I may be resigning. Her response was, "No Gina! I need you! Please, go home and think about it!" I told her that I would, but I knew that I was going home to pray about it. I met God in our meeting place that I met Him in every morning and evening at 6:00 and consulted Him about what I saw in my dream and heard nothing. So, since I heard nothing, I thought it to be nothing, until I went to work the next day and heard His voice. I knew instantly it was God and I was humbled, the fear of the Lord went all through me. I turned to my co-worker who was also a Christian and asked her if she heard anything and she replied "no." It was towards the end of the day and there were no more patients in the office. It was my cue to start tying up loose ends and making sure all the patients had their test scheduled in time for the doctor to receive and review their results before their next appointment with her.

After that I typed my letter of resignation and emailed it to my manager letting her know that this was an immediate action. At the time of all of that happening, I didn't remember that I agreed in June, out of obedience to God again, to be out of my apartment that next week, which was going to be the first week of October. All I could do is sit on the side of my bed in prayer and continue to put my trust in God.

Again, none of it made sense to me. I was a faithful tither, a faithful choir director, praise and worship leader, faithful in my word, and faithful at meeting God at the same time every day. But like I said before, it's always a lesson to be learned, and God was teaching me how to trust Him. I was so use to taking care of everything after my first husband passed away, that I only knew how to trust myself, especially when it came to taking care of my children. I found myself, after putting my things in storage, sitting at McDonald's with nowhere to go until my cell phone rang. God came through again! A kind voice on the other end of the phone said, "I heard through the men that helped you, that you put your things in storage and that you needed a place to stay, you and the children can stay here with me if you like." It wasn't the first place I would have chosen, but it was a place where my children and I could rest our heads.

By December my voice of hope became weary of me not making any efforts in finding a job. She couldn't understand that God took me off my job and that I couldn't apply for another one until He released me to do so. I said to God that I wasn't going on state welfare. He was the one that took me off my job and that I expected for Him to provide, I was not going to apply for that either. It started getting harder and harder to live there before the pressure came for me to move out.

It was during that same time, at my lowest point that God started giving me songs in the middle of the night. I wrote them down and sung them every chance I got, but I didn't know what else to do with them. During that same time, I was invited to go to a Papa San concert with a dear sister in Christ in whom I have much respect for. The night was going great and we were having a blast until this artist came on stage, Chevelle Franklyn. As she was singing Kill My Flesh, It was like God was right in front of my face speaking to me! I knew in that moment that I was supposed to be singing to the world. It was so clear and I was ready to get started, but didn't know how. On the ride back home I asked my friend if she knew of any recording studios. She didn't know of any off hand, but said that she would look into it for me. Other than that, I don't remember any other words being spoken, but the peace and presence of God was so thick that you could have cut through it with a knife. After I dropped her home I was ready to take on the task of getting the songs God gave to me recorded. In January 2007 it was accomplished. Although not professionally, it was something to get me started. My first professional CD was released July 2012 with those songs plus more on it.

By the end of January 2007 the heat was turned up, I had to move or my things were going to be placed outside. I had nothing but love in my heart for the woman who indeed had a huge heart, but was facing physical challenges in her body. I know that in itself was stressful for her. I sat at her kitchen table as God gave me the words to another song entitled "My Prayer" as the tears streamed down my face. Here are the words:

What else do I have to do to get my breakthrough? I've done all I knew to do for my rescue. You said if I delight myself in You, You'll give me the desires of my heart. Lord I need You, my heart is overwhelmed. Give me an answer, please

say that all is well. I know it's all by Your time, but today I'm falling apart, so if you hear me Lord please help my heart.

God almost instantly placed a brother in Christ on my heart and had me to call him. I called and explained the situation at hand, not knowing how he and his wife could have helped me at all. After speaking with him, he assured me not to worry about anything because he had an empty apartment available. We then made an appointment to meet, he, his wife, and myself to discuss the rental agreement. On the day of the meeting to my surprise, they agreed to give me the place basically for nothing until I found employment. I would just have to give them something if or whenever I had gotten any substantial amount of money from anywhere.

February 2007, my children and I moved into a three bedroom apartment that only God could have blessed us with. Immediately I started looking for jobs intensively, but no one would hire me! I knew that God had provided this place for me, now why couldn't I find a job? Can you believe it was a year later before God opened the door for me to work again? Before applying for the job God showed me in a dream me working back at the same hospital I resigned from. Of course I'm saying, Lord, how could that be? I gave an on the spot resignation! I didn't even know they were hiring until my landlord's wife told me about it. I went and applied for a medical secretary position, and during my interview was given a created position that placed me in a supervisory position! Glory be to God! They said that I would be perfect for the job and I got it right on the spot! Can't nobody tell me about my God! Next thing I knew, I was being asked how would I like my desk made and what type of wood did I want it made out of, as well as how tall I'd like for it to be. My pay increased and then I received three raises within three months. Everyone who looked at me cross eyed through my process knew that it was only God.

Through everything I encountered, I learned how to trust God more than myself. My level of faith increased by leaps and bounds and my prayer life went to another level. My children witnessed miracles that helped them grasp a better understanding as to who God is. Although I was no longer able to give my tithes on a regular basis like I use to, before my time in the valley, my stock in heaven looked pretty good for blessings beyond measures which was just what we received. To get a better understanding, I'll break this down in three parts which is called the three T's.

The Tither

This is the most popular scripture on tithing in the bible, ***Malachi 3:10 - Bring ye all the tithes into the storehouse, that there may be meat in mine house, and prove me now herewith, saith the Lord of hosts, if I will not open you the windows of heaven, and pour you out a blessing, that there shall not be room enough to receive it.***

A true tither takes this verse to heart and tithes on the gross verses the net pay of their income, simply because that's how much they believe in what the scripture/word of God is saying.

Most of us have struggled with what God has said and what our bills are saying and we use the excuse that "God understands." I'm here to tell you that He truly does, He understands your lack of faith and trust in what He has promised if you would only do as He says. I've experienced where I had a choice to pay a bill or to give my tithes many times. Because of my choice to give my tithes, I saw firsthand how God met my every need in all cases. For example, I was in danger of having my car repossessed in 2006 along with some other bills that were behind adding up to a little over $3,000. I was a faithful tither and maintained an intense prayer life. I was able to hear the Lord when He gave the instructions for my children and I to go on a seven day fast.

Seven days straight I fasted with only water and herbal tea without sugar. My children were on vacation from school that week and fasted a half day ending each fast day by reading Hebrews chapter 11 in its entirety. I would wake them up before I went to work and call home every day at 12 noon to make sure they read the chapter before breaking their fast for the day. As each day passed I was in thought of not knowing how God was going to do it. I just believed with all of my heart that I would get the funds that would help get us out of that financial hole.

Well, I can testify that on the seventh day God laid upon my heart to check the mailbox at my old address in Bridgeport. I was at work, so I called my cousin and asked her to take my oldest daughter by there so that she could check the mailbox. Lo and behold, my daughter called me from our old address with pure excitement in her voice telling me that I had several checks in the mail! I didn't know the amount at the time, I only knew within myself that it would be enough for me to pay my bills. My cousin brought my daughter to my workplace to hand the checks over to me, and when I calculated the amount of each check it addd up to a little over $4,000! Look at my God! I was able to pay my bills, give my tithes that were due off of the money that He blessed me with, and I had some left over for all of us to enjoy and save.

The bible says in **Isaiah 1:19 - *If ye be willing and obedient, ye shall eat the good of the land.*** But it also gives warning in verse 20 saying; ***But if ye refuse and rebel, ye*** *shall be devoured with the sword: for the mouth of the Lord hath spoken it.* We all know that God wasn't talking about tithing per say in those scriptures, but disobedience is disobedience. He tells us to bring our tithes and offerings to the storehouse, He didn't say to bring them if we wanted to. He gave us instructions and then promises, because He is God and is able to make good on his word. In **Malachi 3:11** *He promised that He would* **rebuke the devourer for your sakes and shall not destroy the fruits of your ground; neither shall your vine cast her fruit before the time in the field, saith the Lord of host.** And then in verse 12 He says; ***And all nations shall call you blessed: for ye shall be a delightsome land, saith the Lord of hosts.*** Listen, this is a guarantee! You can't go wrong!

God commanded us to give ten percent of our wages, but just because He commands us to give money doesn't mean that we can't receive money from Him. We are literally afraid and think it's a sin to ask God for money and will go lacking. But in ***Ecclesiastes 10:19*** it reads, ***A feast is made for laughter, and wine maketh merry: but money answereth all things.*** So it's okay to ask God for funds or money as long as you don't obsess over it because it's the love of money that is the root of all evil. *(Timothy 6:10)* The other responsibility that comes along with being a tither is that we must be good stewards over our money so that we can have something put away for a rainy day as the saying goes. It reads in ***Proverbs 13:22 – A good man leaveth an inheritance to his children's children: and the wealth of the sinner is laid up for the just.***

When God blesses you, especially financially, it's not just for you only. It is to be dispersed as He gives instructions as to how and/or who to give it to. We must be good stewards over what God gives to us, but at the same time selfishness has absolutely no place in the Kingdom.

2 Corinthians 9: 6-7 - But this I say, He which soweth sparingly shall reap also sparingly; and he which soweth bountifully shall reap also bountifully. 7) Every man according as he purposeth in his heart, so let him give; not grudgingly, or of necessity: for God loveth a cheerful giver.

~~~~~The Trust~~~~~

Trust is the assured reliance on the character, ability, strength, or truth of someone or something. It's also one in which confidence is placed and dependence on something future or contingent; Hope.

We have all been let down at some point in our lives, but in Christ we can find this type of trust. He will even go to the extent of proving that He's trustworthy by allowing you to fall into difficult circumstances that only He could bring you out of. This may seem like a cruel thing to do, but how will you know that He can rescue you out of the deep sea if you never drowned?

King Jehoshaphat was afraid when he heard that the children of Moab, Ammon and mount Seir wanted to go up against him in battle. Although he feared, he knew where his help came from. He called a fast throughout Judah and they sought the face of the Lord concerning this matter. God heard the cries of His people and spoke through His servant Jahaziel to King Jehoshaphat saying; **Be not afraid nor dismayed by reason of this great multitude; for the battle is not yours, but God's. (2 Chronicles 20:15)** Then God began to give instructions, remember that God will always give instructions before your victory is manifested. And if you truly trust Him you will carry them out no matter how insane it may sound. I'm sure that in the word given by the prophet Jahaziel, King Jehoshaphat felt confident that God was with him. If he didn't he would not have responded the next morning as he did.

2 Chronicles 20:20 - And they rose early in the morning, and went forth into the wilderness of Tekoa: and as they went forth, Jehoshaphat stood and said, Hear me, O Judah, and ye inhabitants of Jerusalem; Believe in the Lord your God, so shall ye be established; believe his prophets, so shall ye prosper.

They began to praise God with a knowing that they had already won the battle. Surely as they sung and praised God, He (God) set ambushes against the multitude and they were killed. It was because of their obedience that they prospered greatly in abundance. It was so much that it took them three days to carry back the riches of their enemies. Now won't He do it every time!

God kept his word and the king and his men didn't have to fight at all as He said. They were in position as we must always be, but the only weapon they used was their weapon of praise. That is what I call trust. How much do you trust the Lord? Do you trust Him in every aspect of your life, or are you still trying to hold back some things? I know that you don't understand His ways and how He does what He does, but that's one of the great things about trusting God! You don't have to worry about the details of fixing the problem, you just have to follow His instructions.

We read in the bible about the many different people who placed their trust in God and He came through for them. When are we going to do the same? We trust in other people, our jobs, and other resources, but not the one who is the source of it all. What about when God blessed you with that God sent spouse and the marriage started going downhill? Did you trust God to bring it back together or did you trust in what your friends had to say? What about the house God has blessed you with? You mismanaged your money and were in trouble of losing it. Did you trust that God would help you out of that bind after repenting for mismanaging the money? Or did you fear and started asking close relatives to loan you the money? We must learn to put **all** of our trust in the Lord. I love what David said in ***Psalms 20:7 – Some trust in chariots, and some in horses: but we will remember the name of the Lord our God***. No matter the problem, Jesus is will always be the answer.

The Test

A test, whether it's a pretest or the actual test, always follows a teaching or training course and God does both. He teaches and then trains us so that we are equipped and knowledgeable to pass the test. Please note, prayer and faith will be the key to passing all tests given.

So you went through the teaching and training course of trusting God and He came through for you. Not only did He come through for you like He said, but it was quick, faster than expected and you were ecstatic. A short time after that you get hit with a pretest and again you pass with flying colors, you prayed and held tight to your faith in God and He came through for you again. It took a tad bit longer, but yet you were amazed.

Now, here comes the test. The test is still a situation you can't see your way out of, but the process of coming out of it is a little longer and more intense. You're praying and praying and can't hear nothing from God. You go to church and you can't even get a word from a prophet concerning your situation. All you have is a promise that He will see you through. A word that you had gotten from the Lord somewhere at the beginning of the storm. It would be the only thing that would sustain you when those moments of "where are you God" come about.

All of a sudden when you're just about at your wits end, here comes God. You passed the test with flying colors! All though things looked bad you kept your joy, and when things were falling apart you kept your peace. People told you opposite than what you knew God said and you pressed even the more.

Your faith in that word God spoke over your life helped you to stand your ground and not be moved. All of a sudden your situation no longer spoke to you, but you to it through your words and actions.

For example: you knew you didn't have much, but yet you gave. Where folks tried to ruffle your feathers you kept your cool. Although your faith was shaken you didn't waver, but stayed in the face of Jesus daily. The outcome of it all was awesome! God came through for you once more as you knew He would, and now you are much stronger and wiser to make it through to your next journey.

It's a good possibility that you may be going through something right at this moment. *I know I am.* God has made some promises to me that I have yet to see come to pass and I'm not letting up until I see the manifestation of it all. Jacob said that he wouldn't let go until He blessed him and God did just that. Jacob was persistent as we should be, he wasn't going to let go until something happened. I too will not let go until I see every promise of God fulfilled in my life. Yes, it looks impossible to the human eye, but I know that I serve a God that specializes in the impossible. That's what makes Him a "let me show you God," He will show you that what seems impossible He will make possible that we and others will know for sure that it was only Him.

God wants for us to become more like Him on a daily basis. Jesus is the best example of someone who went through the storms of people rejecting Him, talking about Him and trying to kill Him, all for the sake of the gospel.

Every testimony I mention in this book had a period of testing that took me to the next level in Him. We just have to be the soldiers that God has called for us to be, so that we can hear well done thy good and faithful servant at the end of our life's journey.

Prayer, Faith, Fruition

Chapter 5

The one thing I will allude to throughout this book is prayer because it's our communication to the Father. The meaning of 1 ***Thessalonians 5:17- Pray without ceasing***, is to pray continuously on a daily basis which is something that we should do as Christians. It is the key that opens the many doors in our lives.

Matthew 7:7 – Ask and it shall be given you; seek, and ye shall find; knock, and it shall be opened unto you.

Well, how do we ask? We ask through prayer, we seek in prayer, and we knock through prayer. It's simple, after asking God through prayer for something, we either want to know where it is, who it is, where to find it, or all of the above. So what do we do? We begin to seek God through prayer for those answers. After seeking, God will show us which avenue to go down to obtain what it is that He has granted us so that we can now have it. This is most likely where faith steps in, another tool I will allude to throughout this book. Our faith is what moves God and without it we cannot please Him.

Matthew 17: 20 - And Jesus said unto them, Because of your unbelief: for verily I say unto you, If ye have faith as a grain of mustard seed, ye shall say unto this mountain, remove hence to yonder place; and it shall remove; and nothing shall be impossible unto you.

I personally rejoice in the last portion of that verse…"NOTHING" shall be impossible unto you. That challenges a person to exercise their faith because God cannot go back on His word. Again,

Numbers 23:19 – God is not a man, that he should lie; neither the son of man, that he should repent: hath he said, and shall he not do it? Or hath he spoken, and shall he not make it good?

That scripture by itself is enough to increase ones faith! That means I can believe the word He has spoken over my life because the bible said that He shall make good on it. Meaning that His word is certainly His bond.

Hannah was a woman of both, prayer and faith. She was also barren which made her a little discouraged, or as the bible states in the amplified version, grieved. It didn't help any that Peninnah, Elkanah's other wife provoked her year after year because of her barrenness. Have you ever experienced people knowing that you're in need of something that they may have accomplished already? Each time they're in your presence or you in theirs they constantly remind you that you still don't have all of which they have already achieved?

Well, Peninnah had children and kept throwing up the fact that Hannah did not. She may have even been a little jealous as most are when they behave in such a manner. Elkanah loved Hannah with or without children more than he loved Peninnah, which could have posed as a huge problem right there within itself.

The bible tells us that when Elkanah sacrificed he only gave Peninnah and her children portions, but gave Hannah a worthy portion, or some may say a double portion. **(1 Samuel 1:4-5)** Hannah was truly favored by her husband. Like Peninnah, people will do all kinds of evil towards you when they see God's favor upon your life. You don't have to have as much as they have or even look as good as they look, they will despise you just because of who you are in Christ and how you represent Him.

Don't you know that they recognize that you don't carry yourself the way they do when trouble arises? You always keep a smile on your face when adversities come up, because you're assured that God is working it all out for your good while they are in panic mood. While you're in peace they are pacing the floor back and forth wondering how they're going to defuse the situation.

So, let's not be fooled by certain things, if you display the characteristics of God, there will be a Peninnah in the midst. Don't worry about searching them out because they are easy to find. Just to set the record straight, Peninnah has no respect of gender. They'll be the one that will show off the new house and/or car they just bought. Let's not forget the new name brand clothes they just purchased, and the man/woman who appears to have it going on that they're about to marry; all as you're going through the birthing process. It may not be all that I have mentioned, but it'll definitely be all the things you have had before God and ready to birth.

They will also be the ones who will hurt your feelings during this time. They're supposed to be your sister/brother in Christ who should be encouraging you through the process, but will say things like; "God wants us to be realistic about what we are believing Him for." "Do you know how much that costs?" What you going to do? Rob a bank?" You don't have to tell me, I know that it grieves your spirit to no end. It grieves you because it's only a diversion to make you stop believing in what God has promised you. They want you to lose all faith in what God has spoken to and over you. Here's the thing, they know exactly what they are doing. They know that if you continue to believe and trust in God that it is bound to happen—you will end up with much more than them. The truth is that you already have much more than them because you have Christ on your side.

Hannah was so hurt one year after being provoked that she cried and wouldn't eat. I don't really know if her husband understood how much it meant to her to have a child when asking if he wasn't better than ten sons, or maybe he did. Maybe he only wanted her to get over the fact that she was barren because of the depth of his love for her. Maybe he just didn't want her to hurt anymore.

Hannah also knew where her help came from and went before God in prayer. She was definitely broken, but yet in her season of bearing. When you're in that season, be prepared to be misunderstood as Hannah was when she went to the temple to pray. Eli was there and saw that her mouth was moving, he thought she was drunk, when actually she was praying in her heart although her lips were moving. Some things you don't need to say aloud! Sometimes it's best to keep your prayers to yourself because people will pray against the very thing you're praying for. Not to say that God won't make it happen for you still, but when you are praying for something specific you don't want that type of interference.

After Hannah explained to the priest that she wasn't drunk, but was pouring out her soul to God out of her grief and pain. Eli told her to go in peace and the God of Israel will grant her petition. ***(1 Samuel 1:17)*** When Hannah heard that there was no longer any reason for her to sit around and continue wallowing in her sorrow. She believed the word that was spoken over her life.

Anytime you come in agreement or line up with a prophetic word, things changes. For Hannah, she regained her appetite and her whole countenance had changed. Her faith kicked in because of the word given by the priest, God's anointed. I believe that she had so much faith that when they got home from worshipping, she was the one initiating the love making. Hannah knew within herself that there was going to be something different about this time around. I'm sure she tried many times before to get pregnant, but this time God had spoken and her faith was put into action. The bible says in **James 2:26 – *For as the body without the spirit is dead, so faith without works is dead also.*** We have to learn how to work our faith, so that it can work for us by touching the heart of God and allowing Him to move on our behalf. Hannah's faith moved God's heart so much that when Elkanah knew his wife He, the Lord remembered her. ***(1 Samuel 1:19)***

Now, let me simplify it for you; when Elkanah made love to his wife she conceived and gave birth to Samuel the prophet. Look at how many times we tried to do things our way without results, until God put His stamp of approval on it. Nothing divine will ever happen when we try to do things on our own; it will always take the super (God) to be placed on the natural for a miracle to happen in one's life.

Once I knew I was ready for marriage and it was unveiled by God, I began praying for a husband with a heart like Christ. God showed me in a dream that I would meet my husband in Georgia, but he wouldn't be from Georgia, but we would complement each other. He also showed me in another dream that he would be a pastor with an established church and a man of valor. Although I rejected both dreams at first, I couldn't run away from the plans God had for my life.

I remember that Friday night after prayer service coming home to fall on my knees again because I didn't understand all the craziness that had broken out in my life. That night I realized that I was getting whipped by God for rejecting his plans for me. After repenting I took the first step and accepted with my mouth that I would obey His will for my life and marry a pastor. It was a huge step for me, I was always afraid of the blood of others being on my hands as a child growing up. Being a pastor's wife was not my forte, but I was willing to be taught and trained by God as he did for me as a choir director. It wasn't until a couple of years later that I accepted it in my heart after moving to Georgia.

There's a difference in accepting something with your mouth and accepting it with your heart. Like forgiveness, it's a step by step, day by day process. However, at some point I began to get weary because it seemed as though it would never happen. All of these counterfeit preachers kept coming my way, I had just about enough. Not only was I tried of being sick and tired, my Peninnah which was more than one person, was on the scene. They flashed their relationship all in my face. They made me feel like a pastor/preacher would never look my way, because I didn't have what it took to be such a wife in their eyes. This one person even said that they saw God sending me a psalmist like myself so that we could sing the praises of the Lord together. To say the least, I was hurt and started second guessing what I knew deep in my heart God had shown me.

Then the "woe is me" prayers began. It went a little something like; "God, you know I didn't ask for a pastor as a husband. I would have been alright with just having someone who loved You with all his heart and followed after your ways. So why did you show me that I would marry a pastor—when Your plans are to send me a Psalmist?"

Trust me, I went on and on and on…. my heart was broken and my faith had weakened…But God. He confirmed that the dream He gave me was definitely from Him and even gave me the first name of my husband. I didn't realize it until after we got married before God brought it to my attention. But it's not everything He allows us to unravel, some things must be revealed at an appointed time.

The first thing I did after getting the revelation that folks were trying to kill my promise, desire, and destiny was to cut off the Peninnahs in my life. It no longer mattered to me what title they held, I had an understanding that they didn't feel like I was on their level and didn't deserve someone of their "status." I also had an understanding that they were on assignment to sabotage God's plan for my life… But God!

I went ahead and followed God's instruction in starting a single's group on a social media. I didn't know how to run it for real, I was just being obedient in starting it. Lo and behold I started match making the people of God which by the way turned out very well because of the biblical standards that were in place. I just don't think that is what God had in mind. But yes! It was a step of faith! And yes! My faith was strengthen again! The group gave me the opportunity to pray with the singles and discerning if they were really ready for marriage or not. If they were ready I would match them, if they was not I would counsel them. It was great being able to counsel!

Not too long after starting the group my obedience paid off by getting introduced to my husband. I had already said to God that I wouldn't marry anyone that came through the Single's ministry and He knew my heart was set against that. He is such a God of wisdom! He used a mutual friend of ours who suggested that he would be a great asset to me in running the ministry.

All I can tell you is that the first week we met we talked all day every day on the phone about our whole lives just about, the good, the bad, and the ugly. Week two was the week of confirmation for the both of us. God confirmed our union through dreams we had way before meeting each other. In fact, we had the same dream at different times of our walk in God. We even met in Georgia as one of my dreams indicated! At the end of week one on a Saturday he said that we must meet each other face to face and of course I was in agreement with it. I didn't know he was actually looking for airfares at the time of us discussing it. After he made sure of my days off and I agreed to meeting him one day soon he said that he clicked the submit button that book his fare.

After finalizing his flight he then gave me his itinerary for the following day after getting off of work that morning. He said that he would leave work and go straight to church because he could shower and get dress for Sunday service there. He'd have dinner with his parents as he did every Sunday after church, go home and pack and then catch a red eye out to Atlanta. After all of that he then said that he would be free to meet me anywhere I'd like to meet Monday morning if I was willing. He made sure to tell me that we only had that one day because he would leave out first thing Tuesday morning. I was so shocked! At that time Sunday, Monday, and Tuesday were my days off, so I had no excuse so I agreed.

At the end of week two he proposed and we were married on that Friday of week three and are still happily married today. Now, what if I would have listened to my Peninnahs? If I had listen, none of what God had showed me would have come into fruition. We have to know that God speaks to us too. I know that I was only a "Psalmist" at the time, but I was a psalmist that had a strong prayer life and relationship with God who knew when God was speaking to her. But sometimes we get intimidated because of folks titles.

We think because they sometimes say the right things at the right time that they have our best interest at heart, but they don't. They want to stay close enough to give you false hope and discouraging words that sound good because they have an inclination of who you will become in the Kingdom for the glory of God. Most are just afraid of being out grown spiritually and will try to stop you from reaching your destiny at any cost. But what if they only had the mindset of the Kingdom? Kingdom minded people would help you achieve all that God has ordained for your life, with the understanding that we all have a part to play. It doesn't matter if your part seems to bigger than my part or vice versa, the importance is that it will all benefit the Kingdom of God. What may sound funny to some is that I still speak to all of the individuals and genuinely love them. Yes, I cut them off, off from knowing the rest of God's plan for my life, because I was able to clearly see their spirit and understood that they needed deliverance in that particular area in their life—nothing personal.

What I mainly love about Hannah is that although she lost her appetite and her joy, she didn't lose her self-respect. She showed herself to be a true woman of God by being angered, but sinning not. Something I can assure you of is this; if we don't act out in God, we will surely act out of our emotions. Hannah could have easily laid down all that she was in Christ and cussed Peninnah out as some of us may have, but she decided to remain holy and pray. Hannah put in practice self-control, long suffering, and temperance as we would need to in our Christian journey.

Good Seeds/Bad Seeds

Chapter 6

The bible says in ***James 3:16 – For wherever there is jealousy (envy) and contention (rivalry and selfish ambition), there will also be confusion (unrest, disharmony, rebellion) and all sorts of evil and vile practices. Amp version*** I know that most of us have experienced being envied at one time in our lives or another, especially in this day and age. People envy you mainly because you possess something they long to have like a position at work, a brand new vehicle, a good husband or wife, a beautiful home, the personality you obtain, etc. Surprisingly so, the majority of these people are found right in our own families or close circle. Because we know there's nothing new under the sun, ***Ecclesiastes 1:9***, let us look at a woman in the bible who envied her sister greatly.

We have all looked at Rachel as being the beautiful one, but have you ever notice how envious she was of her sister Leah? Indeed, Rachel fertilized her ground with envy when she realized she was barren and her sister was able to have children. She never thought about how her sister always lived in her shadow because she was considered the beautiful one and was focused on that. It never crossed her mind twice that her husband loved her more than Leah. That he didn't give Leah the proper love or time that a wife is entitled to. It was all about her. It says in the bible that Leah was hated **(Genesis 29:31)** and that's why God opened her womb. She was what we call today the black sheep of the family, used, abused, and excused.

I remember when my mother told me that she wasn't going to buy me anymore school clothes or supplies at the age of 13. I too felt like, at that moment, the black sheep of the family. But I stood up for the truth so it didn't matter. My stepfather violated me and I wasn't going to say anything different from what I knew was the truth. At that point I decided to work under one of my older sister's name at a temp agency for the summer. Can you imagine a 13 year old working at a factory? Well I did and was able to buy all that I had needed plus more. It's a prime example of when life throws you lemons to make lemonade and that year I made a whole pitcher full. That year it was pure havoc in the house. I started acting out first by telling people in the church what was happening to me in our home and they of course started inquiring. My mother tried to make me believe her truth, so that her image wouldn't be blemished in the church. I couldn't do it because her truth implied that I was confused about the affection shown toward me by my stepfather. She wanted for me to believe that I was making it all up when in fact she knew that I wasn't the first of her girls that it happened to. Since I didn't comply with the lie, I was treated as if I was no longer her daughter, but someone who she picked up off the streets. My mother was more concerned about her name than the welfare of her child and indeed turned my other two siblings who were in the house, at the time, against me. I felt like an outcast and started to rebel in other ways like running away and talking back when I felt pushed against the wall. I thank God that it all wasn't in vain. I understand today that it was all a process that I had to go through to help make me into who I am today.

Like my mother, Rachel was selfish and only thought about herself. Her attitude towards her husband was even displeasing after she saw that her sister had birthed four children so far and she had yet to birth the first.

Genesis 30:1 – And when Rachel saw that she bare Jacob no children, Rachel envied her sister; and said unto Jacob, Give me children, or else I die.

Wow, "Give me children, or else I die" sounded alternatively demanding to me….

Genesis 30:2 – And Jacob's anger was kindled against Rachel: and he said, Am I in God's stead, who hath withheld from thee the fruit of the womb?

My God! I'm sensing a lover's quarrel right here! But Jacob was right, he was doing his part and everything was functional on his end because he had children with Leah. Only God can open and close the womb, he had no control over that. I believe Rachel knew that her approach was all wrong because in verse 3 she had seemed to have come up with a solution. As you know, most times we women always have a plan, especially when we want our way or to outdo somebody. Rachel's solution was to give Jacob her handmaiden so that she could have children for them through her womb. The spirit of competitiveness has now crept in and is now fertilizing her ground as well.

It's just like today's society of always wanting to keep up with the Jones'. The Jones got a BMW so I'm going to get a Mercedes. The Jones got a 4 bedroom house with 3 bathrooms. I'm going to get a 6 bedroom house with a bathroom in each bedroom. Those are the type of things we do when we're trying to outdo one another. You see this spirit in the church as well as in the world and God is not pleased.

Exodus 20:17 - Thou shalt not covet thy neighbour's house, thou shalt not covet thy neighbour's wife, nor his manservant, nor his maidservant, nor his ox, nor his ass, nor any thing that is thy neighbour's.

Covet: To desire what belongs to others inordinately.

Rachel was so selfish that she even wanted the mandrakes that Ruben picked for his mother.

Genesis 30:14-15 - And Reuben went in the days of wheat harvest, and found mandrakes in the field, and brought them unto his mother Leah. Then Rachel said to Leah, Give me, I pray thee, of thy son's mandrakes.

Mandrakes are an herb that promotes conception. I can understand why she would have wanted them. Was it not possible for her to have sent someone to pick some for herself? Again, it was all about Rachel and what she wanted. Like her father, she was being manipulative when she negotiated the mandrakes for Jacob's time spent with Leah. So in other words, Leah paid for her own husband's time in exchange for the herb her son picked for her. Rachel still knew in her heart that Jacob loved her as was, but was still willing to sacrifice him for one night as long as she got what she wanted out of it. In chapter one we talked about tilling the ground along with all of the good seeds that are sown that will produce a good harvest in due season. At this point, nothing good was being sown into Rachel's ground. The fruit of the Spirit was not displayed in her life at all.

We see marriages of manipulation all the time. The marriage happened either out of convenience or for the love of money most times. In any case, these marriages are barren or lacking the ingredients needed for a strong, solid, healthy, and loving union.

First of all, Christ is not the focal point of the marriage. You can notice this during all of their conversations of the I, I, I's and the me, me, me's. They've done nothing wrong in the marriage, but tried to make it work. They contribute nothing negative, but remained positive and hopeful throughout the whole union and all the fault is placed on the other person.

My second marriage was all about the money and what he could do for me. The difference was that he wasn't blindsided about it because we put all of our cards out on the table before we said I do. I told him that I didn't love him and that I had just gotten out of a bad relationship and all I needed was someone to help me get back on my feet. He said that because he loved me that I would learn to love him and in the meantime he didn't mind waiting for that to happen. We agreed and it was a go, we got married within four months of knowing each other and he definitely kept his end of the bargain.

Unfortunately my eyes kept getting bigger and bigger and I kept wanting more and more. So what did I do? I played the game of manipulation. When I wanted something expensive I would make like he was truly the love of my life and that I couldn't live without him. I said all the right things, dressed a certain way, and made the evening worth his while. How misleading, but I got what I wanted including the big beautiful house with the pool in the back yard and the nice car. Any other time I couldn't stand for him to be anywhere around me. I'm not saying that he was mister perfect, but what I am saying is that in his heart he truly loved me and wanted to please me at any cost. To all of the "getting over people" reading this book, I'm here to tell you that it does come to an end. The other person does get tired at some point.

Now, I wasn't saved during this time, but knew better than to marry a Muslim being raised as a Christian. So what I'm saying is that the marriage was a no go from the start, but it hurt terribly when he asked for a divorce. Even though I treated him wrongly, I didn't want the divorce at all because I strongly believed marriage was til death do us part.

Yes I did the basics like cooking, cleaning, and making sure the clothes were washed, dried, folded, and put away, etc. But when it came to the matters of the heart, my heart was off duty. Even with knowing that, it didn't stop me from begging and pleading for him not to go through with it, but it wasn't happening. I even told him that I loved him and thought that I meant it for real, but I was only in love with what he could do for me. That is what I was really trying to hold on to. No matter how sour the relationship got towards the end, the reality of it all was that it was bound to fail from the beginning. Another life lesson learned underneath my belt.

I had already experienced losing my first husband through a natural death, and now I was about to experience losing one through a spiritual death. To be real honest, the marriage was dead spiritually from the beginning because it wasn't producing anything good. Everything was false. False love, joy, peace, meekness, long-suffering, temperance, gentleness, goodness, and faith.

Even after the divorce he still wanted for us to date to see if we could try to marry again at some point. We did for a little while, but I couldn't deal with the whole idea of being with someone I didn't love. I ended up going my separate way hoping that love would find me again. Needless to say, that landed me into another mess, but I thank God that I found Jesus on my road to Damascus.

Rachel is the perfect example of how we will do anything to get what we want when we're not working with the right fertilizer….. But God.

Now, I don't know what happened with Rachel between verses 15-21, but I can only imagine that a change took place. I believe that somewhere in between there she tilled her ground. She cut down envy, chopped up competitiveness, and turned the ground over and began to plant good seeds that were fertilized with trusting God, having faith, while asking God to forgive her for her actions and previous behavior.

I have this theory because in verse 22 God remembered her and she gave birth to a son. God hates sin and will not bless you in abundance in your mess. In fact, I don't know of anyone in the bible that He blessed at all without them asking for forgiveness. There must be a turning point of repentance that must take place before we can reap the full harvest.

Physical Barrenness

Chapter 7

Many are suffering right now from some type of sickness or disease that the doctor said you will have to live with for the rest of your life. Depending on the diagnosis, the rest of your life could be very short lived. In any case one's life would change dramatically.

They're stressed out with not knowing what's going to happen to them from day to day, and/or about getting their affairs in order. The ones who don't know Jesus may not know that He's a healer, but the ones that know Him should know that He is the "Great Physician" and that they can go to Him for a second opinion. His diagnosis will always be "By my stripes you are healed". *(Isaiah 53:5)*

The problem with Christians these days is that we don't really believe. We say that we have faith, but that type of faith only reaches as far as we can see. That is not the faith that the word of God speaks of.

Hebrews 11:1 – Now faith is the substance of things hoped for, the evidence of things not seen.

But I like how the amplified version breaks it down:

Now faith is the assurance (the confirmation, the title deed) of the things [we] hope for, being the proof of things [we] do not see and the conviction of their reality [faith perceiving as real fact what is not revealed to the senses].

This type of faith has everything to do with your healing, your physical barrenness.

In November of 2013 the nurse practitioner diagnosed me with anemia. It was said that I wasn't very far from needing a blood transfusion. About a year before that I was in a service and the preacher prayed for me and said that I was healed from that blood condition. Well, I didn't know that I really had such a serious condition at that time and didn't think to follow up on it right away. Fast forwarding to November 2013…, before I even went for my yearly checkup it was placed into my spirit to start eating only fruits, vegetables, and fish. I had mentioned it to my husband one morning and started that very day before ever going for my yearly check-up. The nurse put me on iron pills. I started looking for every source of iron to put into my body to help bring my blood count up. While trying to deal with that, another nurse was trying to convince me of being hypertension borderline when I was only there for my sinuses.

God then began to deal with me concerning my body being His temple and all of the unhealthy foods I was putting in it. Although my pressure was up due to an infection from having a dental procedure, it was still a wakeup call. Thank God the nurse gave me antibiotics for the sinuses because it actually killed the infection. That's what you call killing two birds with one stone!

However, I started exercising right away and eating much healthier and lost about 40 lbs. By February of 2014 my blood count was normal and I was giving God all the thanks. I thought about how big of a God we serve and said to myself that I rather not take an iron pill for the rest of my life. So, I bought multi-vitamins thinking that it would solve the problem and at the same time was slacking up off of my vegetables. I didn't do too poorly when I went for my yearly checkup in November of 2014. My blood count was just a bit under normal and that could have been due to that time of the month.

However, I started taking my iron again because I didn't want to face bigger problems down the road. One day it dawned on me that I wasn't taking in the proper amount of vegetables! I knew that was nobody, but God giving me the same revelation He gave me the year before when He said to eat vegetables, fruits, and fish. Like most of us, we only grasp just enough of the revelation to get us out of the danger zone and then slowly but surely get away from the plan. I have now begun juicing my veggies and am feeling great! I am healed! Sometimes our healing comes through just being obedient, but we have to have the faith to believe that God is going to do it regardless of how it may happen.

I know that there are others suffering from more severe sicknesses, but God's word still remains true. Let's look at the woman with the issue of blood mentioned in **Luke 8:43-48**. This woman suffered with this sickness for twelve years the bible said! Can you imagine that? I guess some of you that are reading this book right now who has been afflicted in your body for some time can relate.

The bible also says that this woman spent all of her life savings on doctors who couldn't find a cure for her condition. Her only hope was Jesus. After all, I'm sure she heard of all the miracles, signs, and wonders that followed Him and thought to herself, if I could only get close enough to Him… I'm sure she got word that He was passing somewhere near and made up her mind that this day would be the day I will be healed. On this very day a miracle will be performed in me. Her faith was already increased because of what she knew of Him.

She had gone too long with this blood condition, and I could just imagine, she was tired of just being sick. Nothing was going to stop her that day! It didn't matter the distractions that may have come her way, she had purposed in her heart that healing will be hers that day. That's exactly what we have to do. We have to purpose in our heart that no matter what the doctor has said, you know what Jesus is saying.

You know that He is a great big God that does great big things and will perform the miraculous in your life. It doesn't matter what the sickness is, be it AIDS, Cancer, Arthritis, MS, Sickle Cell Anemia, Hypertension, Diabetes, Renal Failure, etc. God can rid you of all of your infirmities. He can heal you indeed if you just believe. I could envision the crowd that must have surrounded Jesus. A massive amount of people who heard of Him and came out for healing of some sort as well.

I could also imagine the press that was in this woman's spirit. She saw that the odds looked like they were against her in getting to the one who could set her free so she was determined. She had to have gotten close enough to see Him being that she touched the hem of His garment. I can see her on her knees and stretching her body while extending her arms touching the hem of His garment. Just as she pressed through the crowd, we must press through and touch Him through our prayers…He will respond. He knew someone had touched him because He asked the question, "Who touched me?" He hears and feels your prayers and you will know when you have touched Him with them. It doesn't matter how many prayers are going up, He knows you, He knows your voice, He created you. In the passage Jesus knew that virtue had gone from His body, and although He asked who touched him, He knew exactly who it was. It was a must that she came forth and confessed to everyone that she was healed.

Luke 8:47 And when the woman saw that she was not hid, she came trembling, and falling down before him, she declared unto him before all of the people for what cause she had touched him and how she was healed immediately.

Don't be afraid to speak aloud your confession of healing. Let the devil hear you as well as all of the disbelievers. Your God is a healer! He is the great Physician!

Now I know that some sickness just happens. You ate right and exercised, but still came down with some known or unknown disease. Well, maybe you were just chosen for a miracle. It doesn't stop God from healing you.

There are others that are preventive if we would just eat right and exercise. You remember earlier I shared with you about the anemia, but here's the thing…knowing that our bodies were made to respond to the natural foods that are grown, I should had been eating my green vegetables. If I had, I would not have been faced with such an issue. We are a fast food generation that's always on the go. We never make time for home cooked meals anymore because in our minds there's a McDonalds down the street and we can just pick something up there to save time. The grease from these foods are clogging up our arteries and it's causing major vascular problems amongst other things.

Water is also a necessity. I know that I was one of those people who said I couldn't drink water, but I find myself drinking it now because I know that my body can't function properly without it. I eat less starches and sweets and eat more of the healthy foods that are beneficial to the body.

Exercise helps to keep the blood circulating and body toned. We need to keep our muscles built up and strong, so the right amount of Calcium and Vitamin D is necessary to keep our bones good and healthy. It will help prevent Osteoporosis as well as other bone sicknesses. I guess you may be asking yourselves if I'm a doctor, and the answer is no. We all should know the basics of keeping our bodies healthy, especially as we grow older.

Cut down on the salt and watch your sodium intake. Let's read the nutrition labels when we're shopping to help calculate how much of what is going into our temple that we are responsible for. We must practice self-control which is one of the fruit of the Spirit. It helps us to be obedient to God's word. And with that being said, it is a must that we watch our food intake as a whole.

Obesity has been running rapid for a very long time and it's time to put an end to it. I, too am still on the journey of losing the weight, but I am determined to get down these 3 sizes and tone up these muscles in the name of Jesus. If you are still on this earth there is purpose in you, a work for you to do that must get done for the Kingdom. You don't want to fulfill purpose half sick in this season… You have too much to do!

Last but not least, rest is very important and is required. I read once that the body helps to heal itself with the proper amount of rest. True or not, it's a part of healthy living. Make a schedule of your daily routine. Write down the time you will get up in the morning and the time you will go to bed at night, along with everything that's in between. My ideal daily schedule looks like this:

- 5am – Pray
- 6am – Meditate & Read the word
- 7am – Exercise
- 7:30am – Breakfast
- 8:30 – Shower, Get dress and start my day
- 6pm - Dinner
- 10pm – Bedtime

Although my day gets a little crazy at times, the first two on my schedule are a must. The rest of my schedule may alter a little, but they still get done during the course of a day.

This may look challenging to some, but I challenge you to make your own schedule and stick to it along with eating healthy. Instead of someone praying for your healing, you'll be laying hands on the sick praying for their deliverance. But should sickness afflict your body in any way form or fashion, just know that healing is the children's bread and you are allowed to partake of it.

The Fruit Bearer

Chapter 8

What are you believing God for? Does it seem impossible to reach, achieve, or accomplish? Well I have good news for you! God specializes in the impossible and is ready to do the impossible in your life today.

Do you think Sarah was the only woman who was up in age and barren that bore a child? Not at all! Elizabeth was also up in age and barren and John the Baptist was born unto her. It doesn't matter what it is, God is a "LET ME SHOW YOU" God who wants to show you that He can and will perform miracles upon miracles in your life if you just believe.

It doesn't make sense to ask God for something and then doubt Him like Zacharias, especially when purpose is involved. There was a purpose for John the Baptist life and prolonging the process through doubt was not expectable.

Don't you know that there's a time and season for everything and when your season comes to bear nothing can stop it? God will cause the mouth of disbelievers to be shut so that what is destined will run its course according to His timing in your life.

Luke 1:20 – And, behold, though shalt be dumb, and not able to speak, until the day that these things shall be performed, because thou believest not my words, which shall be fulfilled in their season.

You may be the least amongst many, but yet you are the one that God wants to use! You're the one that God desires to bring from the valley to the mountain top!

Luke 1:52 – He hath put down the mighty from their seats, and exalted them of low degree.

How many times have you said to someone when a miracle happened in your life, "I wasn't even qualified" for the position, the loan, the Ivy League college, etc., and got it or got in? Yes, that was our God at work because of your faithfulness, obedience, and faith. Noah who built the ark, worked on it faithfully out of the obedience of God because he believed that it was going to rain. Elijah out of obedience told Ahab to celebrate because the rain was coming. He faithfully prayed for the rain because he believed that God was going to do it as He said He would. I'm writing this book out of the obedience to God and I am faithfully working on it because I believe that it will bring the abundance of rain in my life as God said it would.

Throughout this book I testify of many miracles that I have experienced, but none will measure up to the ones that God has promised me in this season. Those other ones were great, but they were more like taking me to another level of faith for the greater things to come. I am in full expectation and am ready to push at any moment! Can you feel the excitement through my writing! I'm hoping that it would make the baby inside of you leap as Elizabeth's baby leaped when she heard Mary's voice. I believe that the Holy Ghost inside of them connected and caused a holy explosion judging by the way it fell upon Elizabeth.

Luke 1:41 – *And it came to pass, that, when Elisabeth heard the salutation of Mary, the babe leaped in her womb; and Elisabeth was filled with the Holy Ghost.*

Are you filled with the Holy Ghost? If not, I would like to share a few scriptures with you to meditate on.

Acts 2:1-4

1. *And when the day of Pentecost was fully come, they were all with one accord in one place.*

2. *And suddenly there came a sound from heaven as of a rushing mighty wind, and it filled all the house where they were sitting.*

3. *And there appeared unto them cloven tongues like as of fire, and it sat upon each of them.*

4. *And they were all filled with the Holy Ghost, and began to speak with other tongues, as the Spirit gave them utterance.*

You may be asking what does speaking in tongues have to do with bearing fruit. Well, it's very simple, sometimes you just need to pray spirit to spirit.

1 Corinthians 14:2 – For he that speaketh in an unknown tongue speaketh not unto men, but unto God: for no man understandeth him; howbeit in the spirit he speaketh mysteries.

Praying in your heavenly language will unlock things in the spiritual realm you've never dreamed could be unlocked, and will also help your birthing process right along. Most importantly we must remember that the Holy Ghost is the bearer of the fruit.

My husband went to his bank one Monday to apply for a small loan of $10,000 some years ago. He went to the bank feeling as though he was qualified, but the banker ran his credit and informed him that he was not.

Now, this is an institution that he has been banking with for many years. He has taken out other loans in the past and paid them back before time. So, you could understand when I tell you that he came home disappointed saying to God that He had let him down. He did hear God correctly. God did instruct my husband to go to the bank. The problem was that my husband didn't wait to hear as to when he should have gone. Two days later the Holy Ghost woke him up after all of his soaking and told him to go back that very day. He instructed him on what type of clothing and colors to wear as well as instructions to only speak with the branch manager of the bank. So he did as he was instructed and went to the bank and asked to speak to the bank manager, but was given to a loan officer. When he told the loan officer that he needed to speak with the branch manager, she replied that she could help him.

Now, this is a good area to point out that the Holy Ghost is not a negotiator. When God speaks and gives specific orders, you must follow them as such. Look at the prophet in **1 Kings 13:9** that was charged by the word of the Lord not to eat no bread and drink water, or return the say way he came. Those were strict orders that had needed to be followed out. The devil will always come to try and detour you from the plan because he's always seeking ways to kill you, your dreams, steal from you your destiny, and to destroy everything concerning you. The bible says that the old prophet, after hearing all of what his sons shared with him concerning the man of God including which way he went, went after him to purposely take him off the path. He found the prophet and convinced him to come home with him to eat and drink with him. Like Satan, he used what God said mixed it with a lie from his lips to take him off course.

1 Kings 13:18 – He said unto him, I am a prophet also as thou art; and an angel spake unto me by the word of the LORD, saying, Bring him back with thee into thine house, that he may eat bread and drink water. But he lied unto him.

I believe that the man of God chose to believe the old prophet because his flesh probably wanted just that, food and water. Because of his disobedience, unfortunately he died. It was the same old prophet who lied to him that turned around and spoke accurately the word of the Lord while the prophet was in the middle of his disobedience, eating and drinking. We need to understand this:

1 Kings 13:19-26

19. So he went back with him, and did eat bread in his house, and drank water.

20. And it came to pass, as they sat at the table, that the word of the LORD came unto the prophet that brought him back:

21. And he cried unto the man of God that came from Judah, saying, Thus saith the LORD, Forasmuch as thou hast disobeyed the mouth of the LORD, and has not kept the commandment which the LORD thy God commanded thee,

22. But camest back, and hast eaten bread and drunk water in the place, of the which the Lord did say to thee, Eat no bread, and drink no water; thy carcase shall not come unto the sepulchre of thy fathers.

23. And it came to pass, after he had eaten bread, and after he had drunk, that he saddled for him the ass, to wit, for the prophet whom he had brought back.

24. And when he was gone, a lion met him by the way, and slew him: and his carcase was cast in the way, and the ass stood by it, the lion also stood by the carcase.

Don't you know that the same person that caused you to fall into sin, will be the first one to let you know that you messed up and missed the mark? Yes, it will be your sister/brother in Christ. You need to know that they too can be used by the devil when they are out of order with God. It would definitely be in your favor to stay focused because disobedience will cost you. Trust who you are in Christ with the understanding that God speaks to you too. You are just as important as anyone else when you're faithfully walking according to His word.

So, the loan officer ran his credit again and of course it showed the same as it did two days ago…, he wasn't qualified. My husband went on to say that that was the reason why he wanted to speak with the branch manager. The lady replied that she would speak to the branch manager herself on his behalf, but God never said that he would need a spokesperson. He simply said no thank you, he could do it himself. For some reason the loan officer felt the need to at least approach the branch manager first to let her know who he was. It was only the devil trying to run interference in God's plan. After she left the room the Holy Ghost spoke to my husband and instructed him to get up and follow her so he did. When he got to the door of the branch manager's office, he overheard the loan officer discussing his file as he entered. When she noticed him she was just about to ask him to wait outside when the branch manager instructed him to come in and have a seat. Isn't that just like God! He will shut the mouth of the enemy every time!

As he took a seat she reviewed his filed and asked how may she help him. He replied with boldness that he came to get his $10,000. The branch manager replied that according to his file he didn't qualify. As he began to explain to her that he had instructions to come and request the loan again, she began writing. The Holy Ghost filled my husband's mouth with the words to say and he obeyed and spoke them. By the time he finished his request statement, she said to him here's your check and these are the terms of the loan which superseded what he expected. She said thank you Mr. Lloyd for your business, sorry for the inconvenience and have a good day. Talking about the impossible becoming possible!

Listen, it doesn't matter what you are facing right now in this very moment. It could be an eviction, sickness, a divorce, etc., God specializes in what seems to be impossible. Look at all of the miracles He performed throughout the bible. He didn't do them just to say that He did it, He did them to help our unbelief. He did say that He is the same God yesterday, today, and forever according to **Hebrews 13:8**. In **Malachi 3:6** He says; *For I am the LORD, I change not*. So why would He change now? For there is no respect of persons with God. *(Romans 2:11)* The same as He did for one, He will do for another, but it would be according to your faith.

The Birthing Process

Active Labor

Chapter 9

Giving birth naturally or spiritually goes through three stages. These stages are Active Labor, Pushing, and Delivering the placenta. Active Labor is when you have gone through the three trimesters of pregnancy and you are now ready to give birth. The pains of the contractions are coming stronger and closer together causing the cervix to dilate.

Have you ever noticed, that when you're on the brink of a breakthrough, it seems like everything around you is breaking loose? Like when you're about to get that job promotion—all of a sudden your co-workers starts talking about you and treating you funny. They're whispering to your boss behind your back all of the reasons they feel you shouldn't get the promotion. Your boss calls you in their office and says they're going to hold off a little on the promotion, just until they look into some things.

Then a couple of days later out of the blue they want you to take a test. They know already that you're qualified for the job, but they just want to make sure you meet all of the requirements for the position. You've worked so hard to get to this point. You know what God spoke to you concerning this promotion. He said that you would get it. But now, what seemed reachable has now become hard to achieve. Not only that, to top it off your child has become sick and you have to take a few days off from work to take care of them. What a position to be put in. You don't even know how well that's going to go over with your boss. The labor pains of getting what God has promised have become intensified.

You're hurt because the same co-workers who said you'd make a great office manager, are the same ones who are now your accusers. You're aggravated because you just earned the degree to get the job and now you have to take a test to prove you can do the job. You're thinking to yourself that you've pretty much been doing it all along anyway, and if that's not enough, now you have to take off a few unexpected days because your child isn't feeling well. My God!

What about when God is transitioning you off of a job to go into full-time ministry! You love your job and you've been there for some time, but God informs you that He has a greater work for you to do for His glory. Your day begins to feel longer as you're thinking of all of the ministerial things you could be doing if you weren't sitting behind a desk for 8-10 hours a day.

You still love your work, but there's a burning inside of you. You're feeling as if the earth is crying out for you because of what God has placed inside of you. Going to work becomes more dreadful. You know that you have to finish the project God has impregnated you with. You much rather be home working on that than to be punching somebody's time clock. As your contractions come closer your supervisor starts to ride your back about every little thing and every day you're ready to turn in your letter of resignation. In fact, your resignation letter is already typed up and dated but you can't turn it in because your book, CD, ministry, etc hasn't birthed forth yet. Meaning, you're not done writing the book, laying down the tracks on your upcoming CD, and your ministry has a few loose ends that need to be tied up before launching. You're just about done and you are in active labor….that's why the longing for being in the field working in God's vineyard has increased. But don't worry, it won't be much longer….you're on your way to the delivery room!

In this stage you must stay focused and in every stage remain prayerful. Distractions will come to try to take you off course because the enemy does not ever want to see you reach your destination. If you would just stay on the path and continue to follow God's instructions, your baby will not be stillborn, but full of life. Remember, even in the labor room you're instructed how to breathe through the contractions, while the baby is descending through the birthing canal, and when to push through them when it's time to give birth.

Psalms 37:4-5 Delight thyself also in the Lord; and he shall give thee the desires of thine heart. 5) Commit thy way unto the Lord; trust also in him; and he shall bring it to pass.

The last part of active labor is called transition. It's when your cervix (in the natural) or the brink of your breakthrough has opened between 8-10 centimeters. It's when things are being set in order for the birthing of your new beginning. You know what I'm talking about..., It's when your shift takes place for the next stage of your birthing process. Trouble is still hitting you from every side, but situations are changing and doors are opening up for you.

You still don't know how it's going to go down or even where you're going to get the money from so that it could happen. This is when you should be calling in the midwives (prayer warriors) to cover you in prayer through your delivery because the pain is much harder and seems at times unbearable. Don't fret because Dr. Jesus isn't like the other doctors, you don't have to call Him in the room when it's time to deliver. He's with you through everything and all stages, and He is ready to deliver what He has placed inside of you.

Pushing

This is a very exciting stage, you are now in the birthing room fully dilated and ready to push. The contractions seem to be a little better to handle because you're able to push through them. You're ready to "Pray Until Something Happens" knowing that shortly you will be giving birth.

When it was time for me to give birth to my first CD I didn't know where the money was coming from to start and complete the project. All I felt in my spirit was that I was to be ready and that everything was going to fall into place soon. Of course people were saying that I'll never get it done. They were only looking at my present state of being—financially, but they failed to take notice of the God I serve. Isn't that just like folks? They themselves will have the means to help, but won't because they're looking to see how you and your God is going to do it without them.

Well, my only plan was to rely on God, which is the best plan anyone could ever have. I remember the night I took my last push… I was speaking with my sponsor on the phone and didn't even know it, and I'm sure they didn't know that they would be my sponsor at the time either! We got on the subject of my music and then the question was posed; "How much would it cost to do this project? "Now, anyone in the music industry knows that it takes a pretty penny to accomplish such a project, so please understand when I say that I was very hesitant in quoting the estimated cost. To my surprise, when I quoted the price the person said that they would love to give me the money as a wedding gift. Look at God! About a week after I got married the money was deposited into my account. By then, as I felt in my spirit to do, everything was lined up. The studio that I used was in place, my start date was on the books, and my baby was birthed in July of 2012, The Road to Destiny. It was done just as God said it would be.

I also remember when we relocated to White, Georgia and the ministry that brought us here could no longer afford to keep up their end of the agreement. They were supposed to pay the rent while I help them start their school of ministry, but that didn't work out to well. The landlord felt bad about my situation and tried to keep the children and myself in the house as long as possible, but it was a difficult position. The bottom line is that his bills had needed to be paid so eventually he had to take us through the eviction process.

My two sons and I ended up living at a hotel in Cartersville, Georgia for about 5 months. I knew that I was supposed to be in the city that my children attended school in because every time we headed in that direction it felt like home. The problem was that it was very expensive to live there and at the time I was only working a part-time job, while in search for full-time employment. I was a woman in waiting during that time, but I didn't want my husband to find me until I was in a place of my own, and if need be, he could take me from my place to his. Whatever way it would play out, I knew that I needed to have my own place first, that was my prayer to God.

Finally my breakthrough for a full-time position in the medical field manifested. April 21, 2011 was my start date. One day before leaving for work I said to my sons to go online and look for us a place in Canton, Georgia and that I'll be looking too at work on my breaks. When I got to our hotel room that night I asked them if they had been looking for us a place. My youngest son replied yes and showed me the apartment he'd like which turned out to be the same one I put on the top of my list that was in our budget. The struggle was that there was now an eviction on my credit report because I also signed the lease with the ministry. But I kept in mind that if God be for me, who can be against me, I made the appointment to see the townhouse.

We viewed it that Sunday, it was everything we could have dreamed of and more. When we left I asked the children if they liked the place and they both responded that they wanted to live there. After praying I called the owner and told him that I was interested in the property and that I would like to fill out the application. He ran my credit and there was the eviction. But because God told me that Canton was my Canaan Land I pushed in prayer because I realized that I was in the birthing room. I explained to the landlord what happened and gave him the number to my previous landlord to verify the story and he did. He called and said that everything checked out as I said and that the apartment was mine. Now, here comes the second obstacle… I didn't have the money to move in! I told him that I had just started working and could give him my first two checks and he agreed. He went on to say that he could tell that I was a good person and that he wanted to work with me. He held the apartment for a whole month for me! Look at God!

When God speaks to you concerning something, you must believe or you may never see it come to pass. In both situations I prayed fervently with the belief that God will do it, and in both incidents He came through for me. Now how much more would He do for you? I would also have you to know that nine months after I was in my townhouse my husband found and married me within three weeks of us knowing each other. Talk about birthing! Thanks be to God, my CD has opened doors for me to minister in song on different television programs, many churches, and events in and out of the country. I'm not sure where this book will take me, but I do know that God will take us to places we could never go on our own, if we continue to stay in His will. The bible says in the Proverbs: ***Proverbs 3:6 – In all thy ways acknowledge him, and He shall direct thy paths.***

It also says this:

Hebrew 11:6 – But without faith it is impossible to please him: for he that cometh to God must believe that he is a rewarder of them that diligently seek him.

How do we seek Him? We seek Him through prayer. I myself like to set a time that I meet with Him every day, He's always there waiting like clockwork. And don't be afraid to fast! It's okay to turn down your plate from time to time…try it and watch the results!

~~~~~Delivering the Placenta~~~~~

The placenta is an organ that connects the fetus to the umbilical cord for nutrients. It's also important for waste elimination. So, let's just say that your spirit is the acting placenta during your spiritual pregnancy. It would be the organ that distributes the nutrients to the baby.

Like in the natural, you would like to eat all of the nutritional foods to have a healthy bouncing baby. But at times we'll go on a junk food binge which makes us feel more sluggish, lazy, and fat. What do you think happens when we feed our spirit a bunch of fear, doubt, un-forgiveness, gossip, and any other type of impurities?

There's a delay in our birthing forth. We have now become; lazy, sluggish, and fat off of our flesh. Flesh will say, "I don't feel like going to the studio today", or "I don't feel like researching locations for the business today"…I'm tired. The next thing you know a whole two months has passed and you haven't done anything more with those things God has impregnated with.

Just how women have a due date in the natural, we also have a due date in the spirit. There are times when we may be about a week or two late in giving birth, so it is in the spirit. The difference is that more than likely we don't know our spiritual delivery date. We just know what trimester we're in according to the spiritual warfare we're facing. God is so faithful that He will still reach out to us in one way or another to try to get us back on track.

Have you ever heard a servant of the Lord warn someone about being behind time? They may have said something to the effect of; "God said to remove all distractions from your life and move forward without delay." That's an indication right there that they have delayed their birth.

In more serious situations we may have what we call a spiritual miscarriage. It's caused by the infectious lust of the flesh we allowed to creep into our spirit that has metastasis causing us to lose the baby. We have made a conscious decision to not let go of those things that have become a distraction to us. For example, during your spiritual pregnancy you may have gotten discouraged by someone who pointed out some solid facts regarding your funds.

They may have said to you that you're wasting your time trying to get your business off of the ground because you can't afford it. In that moment you began to let doubt set in even after knowing what God said about it. Then, doubt then turns into frustration because you're thinking about all of the money you've already invested and you haven't seen any real results with your natural eyes. Before you know it, flesh has taken over. You're having a pity party, that has now brought you down the road of fornication which entangled you with soul ties. Now you're in too deep, blinded, and don't want to come out of it and your vision vanishes away. Right there is where the miscarriage takes place. But God is so merciful towards us that He will most definitely give us another chance. He will sometimes let us wallow in our pity for a moment and then He will pick us up, clean us up, and will impregnate us all over again. Other times you will get whipped back into shape because you're just too hard headed. In any case, He has given you a second chance for purpose to be birth through you.

The best food for the spirit, is the unadulterated word of God, with some praise and worship, and a whole lot of prayer. With that kind of healthy eating, the baby will come out with success all over it and will grow into something great for the glory of God. So the importance of the placenta being delivered after the birth is to make sure that all of the impurities of the flesh have been purged out of the spirit man. Sometimes while going through the contractions our feelings can get deeply hurt. Someone who you thought never would have caused a painful contraction during active labor. We may not know it, but at times it could leave a residue of resentment behind that can affect the growth of your newborn. So after you give birth make sure you do a self-check, a soul searching to make sure that your spirit is intact so that your ministry will grow in the ways of the Lord.

PUSHING

PAST

THE PAIN

How we're treated sometimes while going through the storm can hurt so deeply. Sometimes in a purposeful marriage you may experience going through some bumps in the road. One may feel as if they're not being heard while the other feels disrespected. Both are in ministry, but have been going through these up and down hill battles that have caused a wedge between them. One or both are hurting because there seems to be no understanding between the two of you. You know God has put you both together, but your marriage keeps breaking because you can't seem to get a breakthrough. When you got married the Lord said that through your union many marriages would be restored. He said that your marriage would be unbreakable because He'll be the glue holding it together till death do you apart.

Why wouldn't the enemy attack it through each other's short comings? God never said that your marriage would be perfect or easy, but He will make it good. It's going to take some going through in order to iron out the rough edges, but you have to be in it for the long haul. I'm sure there has been some unforgettable exchange of words between the both of you. You've gone days without speaking to one another and may have slept in different bedrooms for a night or two. You tried to pray and smile through it all, and in front of others act like everything is okay. But the truth of the matter is that the pain is real. The both of you must go to God first and ask Him to show you yourself in the equation. What part are you playing in it all that is causing a negative effect in your marriage?

Trust me, He will show you if you're open to seeing yourself in a dimmer light. After He shows you yourself, get together with your spouse and admit your faults one to the other. Here's a caution, don't be discourage if you're the only one at the time admitting your faults. It's okay. Maybe God showed you yours first, however, don't let it hinder the healing of you and your marriage. I guarantee God will show your spouse their short comings if they are asking Him. They will come to you sooner or later wanting to revisit the conversation and ask for your forgiveness as well. Most importantly, you must make good on what God has shown you by changing your ways.

Also, if your spouse pointed out something about you that ruffled their feathers, you must also change that as well. In all things you want to be pleasing to God and to your spouse. The bottom line is that Satan does not want for any marriage to stay together, especially a Christian one. He doesn't want purpose to be fulfilled in the union because he knows how powerful you both are as one. Let's be mindful of the devil's devices and not fall into the traps he has laid out for us. You will find that once the both of you have worked the fruit of the Spirit in your lives that you will begin to see your marriage blossom.

There's also the pain of being betrayed by your closet friend. You know each other's darkest secrets and blemished past, but they're now saved and delivered from it. God decides to impregnate you with a women's ministry and you are in your last trimester getting ready for the birthing process. Through each trimester your friend was there with you. She prayed, cried, laughed, and even fasted with you when you needed her to. But all through your journey she has watched how drawn other women were to you and wondered why they didn't take to her like that. She helped you pray for them and would even speak a word into a couple of their lives. God placed it on your heart to purchase a building for women in need and you started the process all by faith. He said to you that if you get the building that He would fill it, with not only women, but teenage girls who are lost.

You will obtain grants from the state and money will find you to help fund the program. Your pastor is in agreement and has allowed you to use the fellowship hall until the building comes through. Your friend on the other hand allowed jealousy to creep in and started dishing out your past dirty laundry to some of the women. They began to talk amongst themselves and started to shun you even though you were helping them. You had no clue what was going on, but you noticed that some of the women stop showing up. You shared your concerns with your friend and she acted as if she didn't have a clue as to what was going on. Your spirit man picked up that there was something not right with her, but you gave it the benefit of the doubt. Three days later one of the women call you to ask if you use to be a prostitute. She said that she heard that you were also sleeping with the pastor and that's why he allowed you to use the fellowship hall for your program. You told her the truth about being a woman of the night a very long time ago before Christ, but that was all. There was nothing going on between you and the pastor. You finally asked where she got her information and she called out your best friend's name. As you hear the name your heart dropped and your eyes filled with tears.

Congratulations, you have just entered into active labor. The pain you felt that day was like a knife cutting you into pieces. Although you were hurt, you confronted her in a godly manner. Because of the guilt she acted out of the character of God towards you. You knew right there that you were betrayed by your Judas. Here it is again, the pain is real, but yet you can't afford to be broken for too long. Yes, some of us get to soak in it for a while and that's okay. Then there is the few who must bounce back quickly. You're about to give birth and must recognize that it's only a distraction.

Satan wants you to miscarry, but the only thing that you'll miss is the fiery darts of the enemy! You went before God broken, He instantly healed your broken heart and gave you inside revelation of what happened. God allowed you to know that your friend let the devil use her because of the envy that set in. Afterwards, He gave you instructions to go to her and say you're forgiven. Now that you have followed God's instructions, your girlfriend is then in His hands.

Congratulations once more… You can start pushing; you're on the brink of your breakthrough.

Pain is just pain no matter how you sum it up, it hurts. It's just like falling down and breaking your leg verses a small paper cut. Both are very painful! Yet, one will heal almost immediately while the other will run its course through the healing process. It doesn't matter how painful the situation may be, the first step to healing will always start with forgiveness.

SCRIPTURES ON FAITH

Romans 10:17 – So then faith cometh by hearing, and hearing by the word of God.

2 Corinthians 5:7 – For we walk by faith, not by sight

Hebrews 11:6 – But without faith it is impossible to please him: for he that cometh to God must believe that he is, and that he is a rewarder of them that diligently seek him.

Matthew 21:22 – And all things, whatsoever ye shall ask in prayer, believing, ye shall receive.

Luke 1:37 – For with God nothing shall be impossible.

Hebrews 11:1 – Now faith is the substance of things hope for, the evidence of things not seen.

Ephesians 2:8 – For by grace are ye saved through faith; and that not of yourselves: it is the gift of God:

1 Corinthians 2:5 – That your faith should not stand in the wisdom of men, but in the power of God.

Mark 11:24 – Therefore I say unto you, What things soever ye desire, when ye pray, believe that ye receive them, and ye shall have them.

SCRIPTURES ON PRAYER

1 Thessalonians 5:17 - Pray without ceasing

Philippians 4:6 – Be careful for nothing; but in every thing by prayer and supplication with thanksgiving let your requests be made known unto God.

1 John 5:14 – And this is the confidence that we have in him, that, if we ask any thing according to his will, he heareth us:

Colossians 4:2 – Continue in prayer, and watch in the same with thanksgiving;

Jeremiah 29:12 – Then shall ye call upon me, and ye shall go and pray unto me, and I will hearken unto you.

Romans 12:12 – Rejoicing in hope; patient in tribulation; continuing instant in prayer;

Psalms 145:18 – The Lord is nigh unto all them that call upon him, to all that call upon him in truth.

Jeremiah 33:3 – Call unto me, and I will answer thee, and show thee great and mighty things, which thou knowest not.

John 14:13 – And whatsoever ye shall ask in my name, that will I do, that the Father may be glorified in the Son.

1 John 5:15 – And if we know that he hear us, whatsoever we ask, we know that we have the petitions that we desired of him.

SCRIPTURES ON FORGIVENESS

Ephesians 4:32 – And be ye Kind one to another, tenderhearted, forgiving one another, even as God for Christ's sake hath forgiven you.

Mark 11:25 – And when ye stand praying, forgive, if ye have ought against any: that your Father also which is in heaven may forgive you your trespasses.

1 John 1:9 - If we confess our sins, he is faithful and just to forgive us our sins, and to cleanse us from all unrighteousness.

James 5:16 - Confess [your] faults one to another, and pray one for another, that ye may be healed. The effectual fervent prayer of a righteous man availeth much.

Luke 6:27 - But I say unto you which hear, Love your enemies, do good to them which hate you,

Colossians 3:13 - Forbearing one another, and forgiving one another, if any man have a quarrel against any: even as Christ forgave you, so also [do] ye.

1 Corinthians 10:13 - There hath no temptation taken you but such as is common to man: but God [is] faithful, who will not suffer you to be tempted above that ye are able; but will with the temptation also make a way to escape, that ye may be able to bear [it].

ENCOURAGING VERSES

Have not I commanded thee? Be strong and of a good courage; be not afraid, neither be thou dismayed: for the Lord thy God is with thee whithersoever thou goest. **(Joshua 1:9 KJV)**

And David said unto him, Fear not: for I will surely shew thee kindness for Jonathan thy father's sake, and will restore thee all the land of Saul thy father; and thou shalt eat bread at my table continually. **(2 Samuel 9:7 KJV)**

And it shall come to pass, if thou shalt hearken diligently unto the voice of the Lord thy God, to observe and to do all his commandments which I command thee this day, that the Lord thy God will set thee on high above all nations of the earth: **(Deuteronomy 28:1 KJV)**

For our gospel came not unto you in word only, but also in power, and in the Holy Ghost, and in much assurance; as ye know what manner of men we were among you for your sake. **(1 Thessalonians 1:5 KJV)**

Having made known unto us the mystery of his will, according to his good pleasure which he hath purposed in himself: **(Ephesians 1:9 KJV)**

For, lo, the days come, saith the Lord, that I will bring again the captivity of my people Israel and Judah, saith the Lord: and I will cause them to return to the land that I gave to their fathers, and they shall possess it. **(Jeremiah 30:3 KJV)**

AUTHOR'S BIO

Recording artist Gina Redwood-Lloyd is the First Lady of Deliverance Temple of Faith located in White Oak, NC and Canton, Ga. She is an author and psalmist. Gina is anointed and ordained a prophetess to the nations and she only preaches the unadulterated word of God.

After the long journey from childhood to adulthood, Gina understands what it means to be battered, homeless, jobless, widowed, divorced, as well as being single with and without Christ. These life experiences have prepared her for the road she is now on today called "Destined Purpose."

Her favorite quote is "He's a great big God that does great big things," because she has experienced His greatness first hand and prays the same for women worldwide.

CONTACT INFORMATION

Email address: ladygina393@gmail.com

Phone: 770-549-8181/855-778-4462

Website: www.ginaredwood.org

Address: PO Box 4266, Canton, Ga 30114

www.ingramcontent.com/pod-product-compliance
Lightning Source LLC
Chambersburg PA
CBHW070303230426
43664CB00014B/2620